BERTRAND RUSSELL, A. S. NEILL HOMER LANE, W. H. KILPATRICK

Four progressive educators

Educational Thinkers Series

Bertrand Russell, A. S. Neill Homer Lane, W. H. Kilpatrick

Four progressive educators

Edited, with an Introduction, by

Leslie R. Perry

Collier-Macmillan Publishers, London
The Macmillan Company, New York
Collier-Macmillan Canada Limited, Toronto

First published in 1967 by
Collier-Macmillan Publishers
Blue Star House, Highgate Hill, London, N.19

Collier-Macmillan International
a Division of the Macmillan Company, New York
New York, Toronto, Sydney, Mexico City, Manila

The Macmillan Company, New York
Collier-Macmillan Canada Limited, Toronto

Library of Congress catalogue card number: 67-17504

First printing 1967
Second printing 1971

Set in 10 on 11½ point Times Linotype
Printed in Great Britain by Willmer Brothers Limited, Birkenhead

Contents

Acknowledgements

Grateful acknowledgements are made as follows for permission to reprint material used in this book.

Extracts from Bertrand Russell's *Sceptical Essays*, *Mysticism and Logic*, *The Scientific Outlook*, *Education and the Social Order*, and *Principles of Social Reconstruction* are reprinted by permission of George Allen & Unwin Ltd. Extracts from his *Why I am not a Christian* copyright © 1957 by George Allen & Unwin Ltd. and *Unpopular Essays* copyright © 1950 by Bertrand Russell are reprinted by permission of George Allen & Unwin Ltd, and Simon and Schuster Inc. Extracts from his *On Education* are reprinted by permission of George Allen & Unwin Ltd and Liveright Publishing Corporation.

Extracts from A. S. Neill's *The Problem Teacher*, *A Dominie in Doubt*, *That Dreadful School*, *The Free Child* and *The Problem Child* are reprinted by permission of Mr. A. S. Neill, Herbert Jenkins Ltd. and Collins-Knowlton-Wing Inc. The extract from his *Talking of Summerhill* is reprinted by permission of Mr. A. S. Neill and Victor Gollancz Ltd.

Extracts from Homer Lane's *Talks to Parents and Teachers* and from W. D. Wills' *Homer Lane: A Biography* are reprinted by permission of George Allen & Unwin Ltd.

Extracts from W. H. Kilpatrick's *Philosophy of Education* copyright © The Macmillan Company 1951 are reprinted with permission of The Macmillan Company. Extracts from his *The Teacher and Society* and *Foundations of Method* are reprinted by permission of Mrs. W. H. Kilpatrick. Extracts from his *The Educational Frontier* are reprinted with acknowledgement to Appleton-Century-Crofts.

Introduction

I

Books of extracts are often written to celebrate a reputation, or to move the reader to greater exertions by the words of the great. Neither of these reasons account for the assembling of this selection. For the traditional book of extracts reflects a traditional conception of their role, and below this conception is rejected. Rather, these extracts are thought of as working documents, selected to provide an occasion for critical and reflective thought, and presented in an order designed to ease the strain we always feel when we think warily, acutely, and yet receptively.

The problem of any present-day student of philosophy of education is to see what is the relevance of great educationists at all to anyone trying to think clearly about educational issues. One might surely hold the opinion that what is past is a mere history of ideas considered useful in their time. Should we not therefore relegate them to the attention of historians of education, and go directly to the work of applying conclusions worked out in pure philosophy to the field of education? In this way we could rid ourselves, right from the beginning, of the mistaken and the obsolescent, and apply our present resources directly to our present problems.

This view is dismissed here; not out of reverence for pioneers, but out of a sense of relevance to our subject-matter. Many educational ideas, to be sure, are purely a matter of history. Some are not. We are still talking about them. And therefore because they form part of contemporary educational discussion, they are relevant material for the student of philosophy of education. This opinion, however, will be thought a mistaken idea of what educationists should be talking about by those who argue that the true subject-matter is indeed relevant areas of pure philosophy applied to education. However, we are not solely concerned with what educationists *should be* talking about but with what they *are* talking about. This tangled mass of talk contains many genuine insights by educationists of the past, but it is inconsistent, even haphazard. From it, none the less, many present-day teachers in training continue to seek a faith by which to live. Certainly, the philosopher, like any other expert, can recommend to educationists how they ought to proceed, but he can also render very great help, above all to the student teacher, by giving a clear and concise analysis of present educational discussion.

So writings of great educationists form at least part of the main subject-matter of philosophy of education, and it is not drawn from the heartlands of pure philosophy. It consists of problems provided by educationists and presented more lucidly by the methods of philosophers. The philosopher however does not pose the problem or say which problem should be considered. The picture emerging, then, is of a discussion which is always going on and has always gone on, and it involves educationists, including teachers, in doing things. Some penetrating ideas were contributed to the discussion earlier in the century; for educational problems, like others in society, tend to be with us for a long time. And that is why it is relevant to see what bygone educationists—the four selected here among others—said. The extracts below, therefore, provide raw material for a student, say in a teacher training course, who is at the same time learning something about philosophical method.

This will seem to some readers a view lacking in reverence for the pioneers. The words of pioneers, we shall be told, are not mere 'raw material' (impertinent phrase) for examination and piecemeal rejection by students! These great men, successful alike in theory and practice, are established authorities and are there to be believed. Their function, and for that matter the principal function of philosophy of education, is to minister to the need for *A Philosophy of Education*, with which students must be supplied. From these words of the great, now universally approved, we select what we can *believe* as our guiding-lines, that is, principles of education to serve us in a life of teaching. It is not cool impartial analysis but belief, that is, something by which we can be moved, that should be our concern here. To that end, summaries of the ideas of these people, and some account of their circumstances, ought to be discussed and selected ideas committed to memory.

This view is rejected here, for the following reasons. To begin with, the great educationalists vary very much in the measure of success they attained, in the points of view they adopted, and the types of practical work they undertook. They are certainly not consistent with each other. The student, therefore, presented with their ideas, will need guidance if he is to select from conflicting views and areas of interest; indeed, he is faced with differing conceptions of what education is about. Second, believing what the great said involves assuming that their circumstances were identical with or closely analogous to our own, which is something we cannot suppose without proper enquiry. In some cases it is obviously false and in others true only with modifications. After all, these men strenuously *rethought* the educational situation facing them and refused to take things for granted: should we do less? Third, the view is taken here that beliefs about education are not to be presented ready-made and tailored for all needs. Rather, they are constructed by students, working on the material with an increasing level of mastery, and attaining to something of their own decision after careful and systematic thought, and by the aid of a growing sense of how that thought applies to their experience. Fourth, the committing of ideas to memory as a way of learning anything is inexcusable, particularly in institutions such as those training teachers, which include in their courses discussion of the psychology of learning. Ideas memorized by those who are given practically no guidance in relating them to daily thought and practice are left to lie inertly in the mind, and are conveniently dealt with by being rapidly forgotten. At best they can have an honourable place in the attics of the mind, like forgotten wedding-presents, reverently laid in cloth and moth-balls, waiting for the day they prove useful for living as well as 'intrinsically valuable', and finally disposed of to the collector of antiques.

By this it is not intended to mean, the philosophy of education has nothing to do with belief. But more compatible with respect for students, at any rate in non-denominational institutions, is an effort to equip them with the mastery to discuss aims of education for themselves. Mentally, to be sure, this may be more exacting than learning a set of ideas to serve as beliefs. Perhaps however that is not too great a price to pay for the development of a sensitive, knowledgeable and mature judgment on matters of educational principle, and a judgment moreover that can continue to grow throughout a teaching career. The opinion then advanced here about philosophy of education, in short, is that it provides students with the equipment to arrive at well-grounded belief, but that the actual beliefs arrived at are a matter of personal decision, not institutional policy.

A further opinion worth considering here is related to the previous one. According to this second view, philosophy of education or principles of education (the first is taken to be a more grandiose form of the other) have one area which is home ground, and that is the area of aims. The student needs to justify, both to himself and others, what he is doing. The way he can get into a position to do this is to think over the material presented, and out of the aims he finds there make some of his own.

This may, at first sight, look like an effort to get clear about one's educational activity—the kind of point raised in Professor Peters' interesting discussion in *Ethics and Education*. To make an aim *one's own*, however, is not a step in clarifying an activity or making it more coherent. For we may make an activity clear in terms of its aims irrespective of whether those aims happen to be ours or not, using 'ours' in the sense meant when one speaks of making aims 'one's own'. An ardent evangelist, for example, may teach the neutral form of Christianity prescribed in the religious education lesson. It may be an aim of some persons or institutions that religion should be so taught, though we could hardly call it an aim of this particular teacher. Yet it serves to make the teacher's activity intelligible.

How then can one justify an educational activity in terms of saying, my aim is . . .? Surely only if 'justification' is understood to be something different from explanation of what one is doing. Justification is not a request for explanation at all, it is, as being used here, a request to the teacher to show what he *believes* about what he is doing. 'Aim', then, in the peculiar sense of this present opinion, is a word meaning belief, and as soon as that is clear, the relationship of this view to the previous one criticized becomes evident. To try, then, to become clear about one's aims, and to check what one is doing for consistency with them, is proper to philosophy of education. But it may be repeated, in conclusion, that the question of which aims are *adopted* by the student as beliefs can be left to his or her own discretion, where aims are taken to be equivalent to beliefs.

All this, however, depends upon the attainment of a certain degree of mastery. This is a term very loosely used, as we can see by the number of different things people mean when they say they have mastered French. In the case of philosophy of education, if it is really to be a tempered and trusty tool, always ready to the student's hand long after he has ceased to train, a good level of mastery is necessary, and moreover of a complex kind. Naturally, it is not meant to imply that a perfect mastery of pure philosophy is essential, but rather that one should be reasonably conversant with the kind of reasoning it uses. The complexity however arises because the student has to learn to *apply* his knowledge with skill and judgment. This kind of complex mastery is no easier to attain than that involved in playing an instrument with musicianship, or co-operating completely in team-games, or bringing up children without making a psychological mess of them. Everyone can acquire the knowledge to play an instrument or take part in a team-game, and everyone can bring up children, but to cultivate an insight into the nature of the fulfilment possible in these things is quite another matter. So it is here: the student of philosophy of education, if he is to attain the kind of mastery he will require, needs all the help, theoretical and practical, he can get; and he is poorly helped by books of extracts, complete with biographical summaries, which give no reason why the author was chosen, why these particular parts of his work are worthy of our attention, or of what materials his work is compounded.

Furthermore, when we read these past educationists, the attainment of the right level of mastery requires of us some notion of the exact *standing* of the material. These writers were in part theorists and in part practical workers. From a philosophical point of view, their work is often very imperfect. It is not to be forgotten, though, that their primary concern was not philosophical consistency, nor to contribute to pure philosophy; at best they contribute only to applied philosophy. Frequently they are not concerned at all with philosophy, they are simply attempting to justify practical solutions that work by giving them a framework of ideas. Not thus, we may say, is the kingdom of philosophy to be attained. Nevertheless, successful educational practice *ought* to command our respectful attention, however loosely it is written up; for it is, properly speaking, a part of education itself. Often, indeed, practical success has followed a very intuitive notion of what to do. If, as said above, we dismiss such writing because it is philosophically defective, then we are omitting important subject-matter, deserving of proper philosophical attention. Admittedly, the price of clarifying the material is often to abandon the silk of pure reasoning for the sackcloth of educational discourse. But to jettison such discourse and recommend a fresh subject-matter would involve us in treating education as a branch of applied philosophy. This would be similar to the supposition made by psychologists a generation or so ago—an attitude which it has taken a long time to dispel. For education is not an applied branch of any *one* variety of pure knowledge, but an area of mixed problems requiring for their solution the help of several varieties. It is as much applied psychology or applied sociology as it is applied philosophy. The recurrent supposition that it can be treated as falling under the aegis of *one* variety of pure knowledge, arises as much because of educationists as anyone else. For, in their desire to solve the urgent problems facing them, they reach eagerly after any seeming salvation, and loudly proclaim that education must hereafter be seen in this newly discovered way. The four writers who are before us here played their part in leading us to suppose that education was all a matter of applied psychology.

Another point serving to show what sort of mastery is needed by the student, is that these educational writers want to persuade us to believe in their ideas, so that, to the confusions caused by a mixture of quasi-philosophical writing and practical reporting is added another: the confusion between impartial writing and persuasive writing. It is no mean undertaking to distinguish skilled persuasion from an impartial putting forward of the facts; for those who want to convince us of something can wear no better disguise than that of the impartial and disinterested writer. It is unfair to expect that the student teacher, even if gifted with a nimble wit, can protect himself against persuasion without some training.

The task confronting the student, then, is to master enough of philosophical procedure to examine the educational writing for theoretical consistency and logical quality; enough knowledge of psychology, sociology and curricular subjects to relate what was written in the past to the present state of knowledge; and enough skill in discounting persuasive talk to distinguish wheat from chaff. Even then he is not finished, for in training he is gaining practical experience. And the practice recommended by these educational writers of the past must be closely related to that growing experience. This is an essential means of judging the writings for relevance; and incidentally it shows that practical experience is immediately concerned with the theoretical course in philosophy of education—whereas often a great gap yawns between the two. Only after all this can we really judge the writing of these educationists. Small wonder that students themselves often submit to spoon-feeding if it is offered, and content themselves with 'curses, not loud but deep' against the theoretical cotton-wool passing for philosophy of education. If the present argument is true, then getting a student to read, mark and learn the words of the Great Educators is merely an adventure into an unrelated world, unless the student happens to spot the relevance for himself—an outside chance.

Educational discourse then is an unending discussion, with the nature and rules of which the student is to be made familiar. It cannot be discarded because the ideas under discussion have a powerful and continuing influence on the minds of men. The discussion centres around a number of preoccupying problems, of which the student teacher, for example, concentrates upon those affecting teaching directly. To make sense of the discussion is a technical and difficult art. That it implies full courses and hard work is not denied. But an informed and professional opinion probably depends upon such undertakings being carried through: an opinion, that is to say, commanding respect among teachers and public alike.

This book then deals with that contribution to discussion made by four past educationists. It is interesting to note how long their writing has formed part of the subject-matter of courses, without any precise ideas as to where they fit in the scheme of things. The layout of this introduction and the ordering of the following extracts is intended to try and help meet present needs. First, we see briefly why these four men command attention. Then we look at the role they played and the tradition they were concerned to combat. We note the substantial agreement among them about aspects of education needing attention. Second, we see the importance of four features of the world of their time in forming what they wrote—psychology, pragmatic philosophy, scientific method and the idea of evolution, and we note the purely speculative side of their work. Third, we note the difficulties of re-reading what they have to say, in terms of our present ideas, especially in respect of the shift in the meaning of key words, the commonsense element that slips into the writing, and the structure of their 'theory'. We see that their language and ideas are often treacherously similar to ours, and that very significant differences are thus easily concealed. To treat the extracts like this involves virtually rewriting them for ourselves. Those who think this does violence to the writers are right, if what these critics want to do is to preserve history. But ideas are not necessarily ready for embalming because an epoch has passed. They may have current use and value—more, the battles that generated them may be linked with our present ones as part of the same campaign. To keep ideas in their original context and present them intact belongs to the historian. But to examine them for what is true and false, to locate them in a nexus of present-day thinking and give them a topical currency is the price we pay for using them at all: and this task belongs to those concerned with philosophy of education.

II

The four writers selected here are all of them men whose names first became known for educational experiment in the earlier part of the twentieth century. At that time, a ferment of reforming ideas was already being felt and had quite a history: in Britain and America, not to speak of elsewhere, vigorous and sustained discussion was going on, and the ideas of certain older educationists like Froebel and Pestalozzi, whose views seemed worthy of attention (but by no means, it should be stressed, all the ideas of all past reformers) were drawn upon and taken up. Montessori, a figure of great influence, whose views commanded as much attention as those of Herbart, played her part in shaping the educational viewpoint of all four of our present writers. (It is noteworthy in passing that both Montessori and Herbart were much easier to assimilate in a more scientific view of education than, say, Matthew Arnold.) Many different writers might have been chosen here: to give a full cover of all so-called 'progressive' ideas now current, one would have to quote from a large number of people. The reason for choosing these four is as follows. Kilpatrick may be fairly considered the principal disciple of Dewey both in theory and practice, but he carried Dewey further in both aspects, and his views where they differ are often confused with those of Dewey himself. For example, the treatment of interest in Kilpatrick is more sustained than that of Dewey. Homer Lane, active both in America and England, was perhaps the greatest man thrown up by the movement on the side of personal relationships, though unfortunately he is the least articulate. No account of progressive education in the early twentieth century, as of half a dozen other things, could omit the luminous and provocative thought and beautiful prose of Russell. To Neill belongs the pen of the publicist, the agent provocateur; he is the gadfly of reform, with an intuitive sense of where outrageous ideas hurt most. Of his single self he has perhaps done more than any man to push this strange object before the public in Britain and very widely elsewhere. If to this statement about the four we add that they are four of the best known, this is to say no more than that, as writers or practitioners or both, they are among the able ones and present us with a clear picture.

It is well to try to visualize the situation in which they conceived themselves to be. Above all they were reformers, that is, persons intent upon playing their part in changing an obnoxious practical situation. A tradition of teaching and education was current in their time as at all others. They brought, in effect, two standard charges against the tradition—one, that it ignored, and had been ignoring for a long time, fruitful practical experiment; and two, that a number of new ideas, either already vindicated by practice or likely to lead to successful practice, were being ignored.

No rival traditional *theory* is at first to be found, although something later appears from apologists for the tradition—defenders who are provoked into writing against the reformers. But the reformers have the advantage of the first move in the struggle; and in any case, the true protagonists of a tradition write long before, when that tradition is itself being established. Thus, the tradition attacked by our four writers was one for the defence of which we could cite Thomas Arnold and Newman. The tradition is then at first inarticulate: and it may well be that Oakeshott's view here is very relevant, that a tradition only becomes articulate in certain conditions of decay and opposition. Rational justifications of a tradition would then belong to its dotage. At all events, the tradition attacked by these men, according to their own report, could be roughly sketched under the following heads:—

1. Its aim was to see that a body of knowledge was learnt and memorized.
2. Its method of testing was by recall of what had been taught.
3. The relationship of teacher and pupil was strictly formal, not personal.
4. Attitudes of the pupil to what was to be learned were irrelevant.
5. The teacher dominated in subject-matter, procedure of learning, and discipline. No responsibility was allowed to pupils.
6. The pupil was assumed to know nothing, and was expected to be passive basically.
7. If control were relaxed the pupil would behave wildly, like a young animal.

8. What went on in school was preparatory to serious living, and had no immediate connexion with it.
9. Children were the same at any age, so roughly the same manner of presentation would suffice for a school life.

At this point many readers will be scandalized. Does this, they will ask, pass for a reasonable presentation of the traditional viewpoint? Is such a caricature worth anyone's serious attention? Let us, however, recall to the reader the circumstances of the time at which these four reformers wrote. The tradition being inarticulate, they had to summarize practice as they saw it, and it is commonplace that noble traditions can cloak rank abuses. They were fighting against objectionable *practice*. What is more, they proved themselves able to conduct the practice of education *in a better way*. It does not, though, follow that their account of the tradition they were attacking is a reliable one, any more than it follows that their account of the reasons for their success is to be depended upon. The important thing is that the prestige and panache of their triumph has tended to persuade us to accept as true their account of the view they were attacking. Perhaps we shall never know what is the truth: for first, the practical teaching situations of that day have to some extent lost their hard edge, and second, protagonists and apologists of a tradition, to whom we turn for verification, are no more likely to give a fair account of its weaknesses than are its enemies, as indeed Dewey later discovered to his cost. So, in reading the reformers' account of the tradition they were attacking, we cannot afford to forget not only that men err in reporting their own doings but that they err fully as much in reporting those of others. All of which is to say, that the witchery of persuasion is never absent; and none of our four reformers are strangers to the art. In fact, in the writings of reformers is to be seen faintly delineated a regular procedure: criticizing the practice objected to, supplying it with a theoretical justification, knocking that justification down, and offering a much more full, ample and systematic account to take its place. Now such a procedure belongs not only to logic but to rhetoric, and to sift out the one from the other, as has been said, is one of the tasks facing the reader. Of our four writers, Neill is the firebrand of rhetoric, whilst Russell, at the other extreme, offers a subtle and teasing blend, more logical than rhetorical.

Fully to understand these men, we need not only some commentary on what they were attacking, but a knowledge of the general climate of ideas on which they wrote. In the midst of the struggle for a better educational world, they sought ideas and often embodied them in phrases having the quality of slogans, such as: we must attend to the child's needs. The ideas that caught their imagination differ among the four, but any reader of the literature is faced with a remarkable fact, namely that whatever theoretical angle they approached matters from, they were in substantial agreement about the concepts needing attention. This leads one to conjecture that a central group of concepts characterize the literature of all so-called 'Progressive' writers, because their reading of the existing unsatisfactory tradition led them to a consensus of opinion about what was wrong with it. We thus find them in agreement about the importance of, say, interest, but for different reasons. This has its darker side: they were also in very close harmony about concepts hardly worth an educationist's serious attention—for example, frustration, attention, teaching a given formal subject-matter, or the personal problems of the teacher himself. The most temperate hearing of the opposing view comes from Russell, perhaps at the expense of consistency of exposition; but Kilpatrick, particularly in the *Foundations of Method*, is capable of giving a good hearing to the foe.

Anyone selecting extracts, therefore, finds little difficulty in deciding what concepts to illustrate. They choose themselves. It will, however, be clear from the above that practically no treatment is offered of rejected concepts, however important the student may think them. Some concepts even of the reforming movement are also missing here, because either they were not thought to be so crucial or are more the work of other and later hands: the full discussion of permissiveness in education, for example, cannot be completed from this literature. What remain, therefore, are classical expressions of concepts like interest and freedom, which all students believe anyway are part of the air they breathe. It may surprise many readers to realize how much these concepts had a time and place of origin, and how much they need to be understood and defended if they are to maintain their place in education against rival conceptions.

III

Reformers, then, help themselves on their way by stressing some central ideas which they consider neglected hitherto. To justify these, they commonly refer to theoretical ideas whose origin lies outside education. The reformers however see the possibility of applying them to the explanation of educational problems. The intellectual discoveries of an epoch are perhaps always taken in this way from the area in which they rose to fame, and put to work elsewhere. As education is not a distinctive variety of knowledge, like history or physics, it utilizes a large number of ideas from elsewhere to cope with its problems. However, there is a penalty in such application. It was not, at the time these men wrote, as clear as it afterwards became, that an idea borrowed from, say, psychology is not applicable without further ado in education. For example, if psychoanalytical ideas are borrowed, as they very extensively were, they cannot be used in pure form unless it turns out that education is really a branch of psychoanalysis. And there are reasons for doubting this. If not, the original ideas must be altered—a point seen most clearly among our four men by Homer Lane. Similarly, if, like Kilpatrick, we make considerable use of Thorndike's laws of learning, it is important to stress that such laws are laboratory findings, not classroom findings. They may be modified by any change from the original laboratory conditions. To put them to work unaltered is thus to invite practical failure, or, the other danger, to give a false theoretical explanation of successful teaching. Later students, like ourselves, examining these things to distinguish the true from the false, find a fertile source of confusion in this type of uncritical application. Moreover, education is not like an expanse of ploughed farmland, over all of which the same seeding will produce the same crop. Lane, for example, concentrated on delinquent and disturbed children, but it does not follow that conclusions valid for such children can be automatically extended to normal children. Perhaps the educational treatment of delinquent children is a branch of psychotherapy: that we should have to discuss, but we cannot draw any immediate conclusions for normal education.

At all events, we find that the discoveries of psychoanalysis were heavily drawn upon by Neill and Lane, whilst the antecedents of behavioural psychology were laid under contribution by Russell and Kilpatrick. Both sides, however, attended closely to discoveries in developmental psychology and the psychology of learning, for one of the charges they brought against the tradition was ignorance of these things. These varieties of psychology owed more perhaps to the antecedents of behaviourism than to psychoanalysis at that time, but they were added by the psychoanalytically inclined to their accounts, without much regard to the somewhat different origin. Out of all this a psychology of development continued to grow, and a good deal of cross-fertilization went on between psychology and education, but that is another story.

Along with this strong preoccupation with psychology went a conviction that philosophy had nothing much to do with education. Each time, as with psychology, an area of scientific study emerged from an earlier speculative treatment of the subject-matter—a treatment coming under the general title of philosophy—it was felt that truth was now to be substituted for speculation. This was reasonable enough, but to conclude that philosophy had thereafter no role to play in matters of education was to say the least, over-stretching the matter. For granted that speculation was, and continues in certain ways to be, part of the content of philosophy, it is by no means all of that content. (Moreover, philosophy, in throwing up speculative material about psychology and education in earlier epochs, was performing a theoretical service, and attempting its everlasting mission of sharpening the blunt edge of our understanding, when no other authoritative sources existed to do so.) However, something was left to philosophy; this was the humble role of getting our ideas in order, and a different task, the assembling of all ideas relevant to education in a vast overview, which resulted in books like Kilpatrick's *Philosophy of Education.* The use of the word 'Philosophy' in this title belongs to this older notion of how the word can be used. But it is time to turn to pragmatic philosophy.

Kilpatrick represents the pragmatist tradition of Dewey. Pragmatism, a philosophical movement which contained a strong protest against idealist and metaphysical philosophy, reached its greatest fame under James and its greatest educational application under Dewey. Closely connected with it was the new psychological work of Hall and Thorndike, which was followed closely by James and then Dewey. Pragmatism was a down-to-earth, unceremonious, commonsense approach to philosophy, valuing the useful above all else, completely confident that it had the solution to all difficulties including educational ones, and equating what was good, in education as elsewhere, with what was useful. It was one of the ancestors of linguistic and concept analysis, resembling them in insisting upon reasoning from the facts and verbal reports available, and often throwing up early attempts at concept analysis. Kilpatrick thus shares weaknesses and strengths with Dewey and other pragmatists. Though long ago discredited in its main philosophical positions by the attacks of Moore and Bradley, it continued to live on in education. A curious but interesting fact illustrated by this, as it is in the psychology used by our authors, is that concepts discredited at their point of origin go on being used in areas of application, apparently without consideration of the fact that they have been overturned by the branch of theory introducing them!—an example is the concept of interest as then used.

Kilpatrick has the closest connexion with a philosophical viewpoint of any of our four writers. This statement will appear ludicrous to those who note that Russell is one of the four. But we are speaking of educational writers, not major philosophers. The remarkable thing about Russell is that his philosophy is singularly separated from his writings on education. He did not subject educational questions to close philosophical analysis. The conjecture is ventured here that this happened because Russell shared the conception of education common to his generation of reformers, that it was primarily a psychological matter. He was considerably influenced by Montessori, Thorndike and Pavlov. Russell has many times turned to education, but viewing it rather as a social problem than a philosophical one. Two only of his books are devoted to it, and the second, *Education and the Social Order*, deals with it solely as a social institution.

However, there are two notions, not perhaps consciously borrowed by all of these writers but assumed by all of them to be valid for any educational writing. The first is that scientific method was the proper procedure for investigating all human knowledge and experience. Considering that theology itself was included here by some, education was small beer; and it is not surprising to find education considered as an area of knowledge awaiting the solution that could be given its problems by the use of scientific method. This was expected at the time over a wide area of knowledge, for example history; and hence as psychological discoveries continued to be made, it seemed that the expected day of salvation for education was at hand. Dewey for example was convinced it was, and probably Russell had strong sympathy with the same view. Certainly Kilpatrick follows Dewey without question in this respect. It was widely felt at the time these reformers first were active that the only redemption from ignorance, superstition or a mere commonsense level of action was systematic scientific research; and to show that something was scientifically arrived at was equivalent to showing that it was reputable. Nowadays, when some areas of knowledge have proved extraordinarily recalcitrant, we do not perhaps have the same general confidence in this matter.

The second concept is that of evolution, which was used in several ways. To begin with, it had made systematic science, it was thought, out of biology and kindred branches of knowledge, and had thus extended the boundaries of strictly scientific knowledge. As well as that, it was preoccupying philosophers of various kinds, and producing in a whole generation of writers like Hobhouse, Green and Lloyd Morgan, as was the case with Dewey, interesting theories affecting ethics, individual development, racial development, and the structure of government. In fact, it is only slightly exaggerating to say, that at the time all development was conceived of as evolutionary in pattern. For instance, psychological work on child development thought in terms of laws working to an end of self-realization, greater viability of the race by reason of this, and so on. Evolution thus served to cover the teleological gap occurring for many when religious types of explanation were attacked. For it played a very useful part in providing aims bound in with the nature of the process of living. Our four writers, in their views of the individual and his development, are very inclined, with the exception of Russell, to see some sort of evolutionary purpose in it all. The number of questions begged by this only becomes clear when, as is happening now, the bundles of meanings tied together by educationists in single words like 'evolution' are taken to pieces and the separate pieces examined. Such, for example, is involved in the present ongoing systematic philosophical scrutiny of educational concepts.

These high hopes were carried forward unmindful of the fact that large realms, such as sociology, were as yet unconquered by science or evolution, or at a very early stage: and the outcome of work in these areas was bound to affect education. Thus our four writers proceeded with a very primitive and sparse sociology, and yet they wrote of it with great confidence, as if the new psychological knowledge available for individuals authorized large generalizations about the social conduct of those individuals. Evolutionary ideas about the growth of groups also went forward in a notable default of evidence. These writers then did not ignore sociology but were content with a highly speculative and metaphysical kind.

One should not criticize these writers for not making much mention of scientific method and evolution. For there are some concepts so universally held to be true, and thought to be of such explanatory power, that all discussion based on a doubt of them virtually ceases: *of course* they are the obvious things to use in tackling intellectual problems—basic things, almost like space and time in the philosophy of Kant. In like manner, nowadays, masses of human peculiarities and conundrums of behaviour are referred to the unconscious, which it is felt, enables a sure insight into social problems among others. But when a generation arises which does not quite share this universal agreement, then the situation may resemble that of the student with regard to these four reformers. The great day of extrapolation of scientific and evolutionary concepts shows signs of being yesterday; and education, moving through the cloudbanks, emits again a silvery light which draws attention to its distinctive nature; and we can begin to ask, is education basically scientific? Is it evolutionary? To what extent is it psychological?

IV

The effect of the presence of this very different climate of ideas, when we try to understand the four educationists in terms of those current in our own era, is the complex study that has been mentioned. Expressed with reference to the language in which these things are expressed, particular words, like 'freedom', which labels one of the key concepts common to this group of writers, had a meaning which does not fully coincide with any meaning now attributed to the word. To respond sensitively to the meaning these writers are trying to convey, we have to try to discern the type of meaning their use of the word carried. As with concept analysis nowadays, they often try to do something for us by distinguishing meanings and referring to common usage, but the common usage of their day differs from that found in our own; and the style of their analysis is loose and confused compared with contemporary work.

Meanwhile, psychology of the epoch, at that time by no means so sharply differentiated an area of knowledge as now, had its own uses of many of the terms, and such uses, for example of the term 'interest', do not coincide with current psychological use. Indeed, so mixed up were the meanings, that psychologists of the period, who often ventured into education, could write about it without any consciousness that the terms they were using needed any kind of qualification. One of the major tasks facing the student nowadays is to become aware of the mixture of meanings, and navigate a deft and delicate path through rather unpredictable theoretical waters. All of this appears at first blush as confusion: but confusion often turns out to be an order that we do not at first understand. It would show better insight if we viewed our task as the attempt to grasp, roughly, someone else's notion of how to understand these problems, and then to interpret that understanding in terms of our present approach. If we omit the first step, then we are likely to dismiss as useless and obsolete what may have value if fully appreciated. To understand Kilpatrick, for example, requires a deal of appreciation of a theoretical background nowhere fully sketched in his works.

Another source of confusion arises from what may be called the intrusion of covert commonsense arguments into the matter. By this is meant, that although constant reference to authorities in psychology and the like is made by these four writers, the kind of research required by them to give full backing did not always exist at that point (and sometimes does not even yet). Then, as now, educationists were always straining at the boundaries of existing research, pressing psychologists to produce more in certain directions (not to speak of sociologists) and wanting to apply material not yet existing. The basic nature of a child, the way he learnt particular subject-matter, the way his emotions related to that subject-matter, learning in actual classroom situations were all, for example, matters about which educationists wanted (as they still want) to know more than was available from psychologists. It was a great temptation, and often an overmastering one, for an educational writer, grown knowledgeable about psychological lore and learning, to extemporize in such awkward passes —a device not unknown, indeed, throughout the literature of early growth of branches of science. The status of such extemporization is that of untested hypothesis where it occurs thus in a scientific context, and perhaps no more than speculation where it is a principle of teaching method. Both are reasonably described as refined branches of commonsense thinking. An example is this. Both Lane and Neill took psychoanalytical concepts worked out in situations where there was one therapist and one patient. They then applied them to group situations where there was one teacher and many pupils. Both men extemporized with such success that their findings connect interestingly with later developments in group psychotherapy. But at that stage the ideas these men used were extemporized only. It is not intended, by these remarks, to disparage commonsense or untested speculation which had their place, as we have seen, in the type of philosophy rejected by reformers. These have their place in educational history, as necessary supplements to existing knowledge in a rapidly developing situation of educational change. For such change cannot be restrained in default of necessary theoretical findings. Indeed, the efforts of high-minded and worthy men have borne the weight of educational discussion, teaching methods and so on, in times of widespread theoretical dearth. One might instance some parts of the eighteenth and nineteenth centuries. But if it once be admitted that there is a more systematic way to study some aspect of education—and surely no one will argue that psychology is not so—then more empirical discussion can only last so long as it is not superseded by more well-founded information. Hence the four writers, from our present standpoint, contain speculative elements of which we can at least in part be rid.

A further point relates to the nature of educational theory. It is a phrase often used, and often we loosely refer to the educational theory of writers like the present ones. If we do this, however, it is well to remember that we may mean no more than a mere collection of ideas, looked at as a whole (as the phrase goes), say in the case of Homer Lane, or something of a more systematic nature, as in the case of Kilpatrick. In all cases, however, the structure is very loose in education: often people borrow ideas without it being really clear whether they take over the whole theory or not, as with Neill's use of psychoanalytical ideas. The most precise form of theory appears in logic, mathematics, or in pure science, where it may feature as a compact, interrelated group of hypotheses, some subordinate to others, and the whole composing a logically related structure capable of explaining a wide variety of phenomena.

The nearest we ever get in education is a sustained attempt to apply some worked out philosophical position in detail to education, as is the case pre-eminently with Dewey. Such a theory however, as so often with philosophical systems, contains large elements of an unverifiable kind, and urges upon us a conceptual structure radically different from present-day ones. Apart from Kilpatrick, who inherited the system of Dewey, we have no sustained attempt of this kind among the four writers, though perhaps Neill and Lane might have committed themselves to some standard group of psychoanalytical tenets. It is hard to say. At all events, the consistency possible, in a theoretical sense, to mathematics or science, is not to be looked for in education. This, however, does not mean that incoherent actions and procedures cannot be pointed out and clarified by philosophical analysis. What it does mean, so far as education is concerned, is that ideas bear a loose relationship, and the connexion between them is to be looked for as much in terms of the *problems to which they are relevant* as in some large theoretical structure.

Last, by now the student may think this a lengthy attempt to demoralize him or her. No such matter: what has been attempted is a frank presentation of doubts and difficulties attending the use of great educationists and their writings. These men, however, yield worthwhile things to the trained and careful reader; and the enterprise of trying to understand them is no mere barren theoretical exercise or game with words. It has immediate relation to the kinds of problem a teacher faces, and this is what makes the whole strenuous business worth the trouble.

How the extracts are grouped

FIRST NOTE These groupings are vague and overlapping, as is fitting for the type of concept being discussed. All that a writer has to say on a certain topic, therefore, does not come under any one heading. In each case, extracts are grouped under the principal item being talked about, but not the only one. Examples: many of Homer Lane's views of education are touched upon in the long extract included under self-government and democracy, whilst the longest passage in the book, that of Kilpatrick grouped under interest as a general heading, may be consulted for all sorts of opinions.

SECOND NOTE These topics, as may be understood from the introductory comments, are mainly a mixture of what we would now call psychological and philosophical ideas, with a liberal quantity of speculative material about sociology. They are therefore grouped as follows. Group I is taken here to be on balance mainly philosophical in nature, whereas Group II forms a commentary on the psychological and sociological ideas of these writers. In no case however is the one group thought of as sharply distinct from the other.

THIRD NOTE In each group, different voices will be heard on roughly the same topic, but it is rarely that they constitute what may be called a discussion together. Rather, different views are being paraded before the reader, who will at times (it is hoped) be shocked by the abrupt transition from one opinion to another. Example: extracts under the heading called the role of the teacher. Since there is no continuous thread of discussion, the extracts under the various headings may be taken in any order.

FOURTH NOTE Some topics of obvious importance do not appear at all. What, for example, were the ideas of these writers on what is educationally right and wrong, in an ethical sense? The choosing of some headings, like moral education and character, tend to exclude others, such as ethical ideas. But the attentive reader will find plenty of ethical ideas ready to hand. The same remark applies to other topics not chosen—creativeness, permissiveness, co-operation, and many others. Readers may be more interested in these. If so, and they own a copy of this book, they are invited to take it to pieces and re-assemble it in an order more likely to meet their own interests and understanding of the problems dealt with.

FIFTH NOTE This way of grouping the extracts involves the sacrifice of a general view of the thought of any one of the writers. The reader however could obtain something of this by reading all the extracts from one writer, straight through the book. The theory of any of the writers however, as has been pointed out, is in any case loose.

Summary of the contents of the groups

Group I

1. Shows something of the general conception of education, including discussion of aims, and of the importance attached to scientific method and evolution. *Page* 31

2. The question of teaching beliefs, and how far teachers should get pupils to believe what they say. Some discussion of the evils of propaganda. (The reader is left with the nice question of whether there is any difference between teaching belief and propagandizing.) *Page* 45

3. The training of character, and along with it the closely connected area of moral education. *Page* 51

4. A topic of the first importance in these writings—freedom and self-government from the standpoint of how pupils react to it. *Page* 63

5. Structure of freedom and self-government in the school and thoughts on democracy—closely related to No. 4. *Page* 71

6. Some interesting comment on the effect of competition in education, and of its origins. All four writers were against it, and similarly a very large number of other reformers. *Page* 86

7. A point for judging practical consequences of reforms–proposals about the curriculum. Kilpatrick was a principal authority on project method. Neither he nor Russell disparage curricula of a formal kind as do Neill and Lane. *Page* 92

Group II

1. The role of the teacher, and particularly the view that he is a kind of psychotherapist. *Page* 104

2. A small selection to show the peculiar nature of love as recommended to teachers by these writers. The reader is invited to compare it with love as spoken of in the New Testament. *Page* 119

Key to extracts used

BR	= Bertrand Russell
WHK	= W. H. Kilpatrick
ASN	= A. S. Neill
HL	= Homer Lane
Russell	
OE	= *On Education*
ML	= *Mysticism & Logic*
SO	= *Scientific Outlook*
SE	= *Sceptical Essays*
PSR	= *Principles of Social Reconstruction*
WIC	= *Why I am not a Christian*
ESO	= *Education & the Social Order*
UE	= *Unpopular Essays*
Kilpatrick	
TS	= *The Teacher & Society*
FM	= *Foundations of Method*
PE	= *Philosophy of Education*
EF	= *The Educational Frontier*
Neill	
DD	= *A Dominie in Doubt*
FC	= *The Free Child*
TDS	= *That Dreadful School*
TS	= *Talking of Summerhill*
PC	= *The Problem Child*
PT	= *The Problem Teacher*
Lane	
TPT	= *Talks to Parents & Teachers*
HL in WDW	= Wills, W. D. *Homer Lane* (Appendix)

The number of enterprising and good teachers is legion, and they should be honoured for their original work in their cramping environment—their barrack-style schools. But I say they have nothing to give to me because we are not going quite the same way; on parallel lines perhaps, but we do not meet, because they are in school and I am in a community.

ASN FC 140

Group I

Ideas about the general concept of education

INTRODUCTION

There must be in the world many parents who, like the present author, have young children whom they are anxious to educate as well as possible, but reluctant to expose to the evils of most existing educational institutions. The difficulties of such parents are not soluble by any effort on the part of isolated individuals. It is, of course, possible to bring up children at home by means of governesses and tutors, but this plan deprives them of the companionship which their nature craves, and without which some essential elements of education must be lacking. Moreover, it is extremely bad for a boy or girl to be made to feel 'odd' and different from other boys and girls; this feeling, when traced to parents as its cause, is almost certain to rouse resentment against them, leading to a love of all that they most dislike. The conscientious parent may be driven by these considerations to send his boys and girls to schools in which he sees grave defects, merely because no existing schools seem to him satisfactory—or, if any are satisfactory, they are not in his neighbourhood. Thus the cause of educational reform is forced upon conscientious parents, not only for the good of the community, but also for the good of their own children. If the parents are well-to-do, it is not necessary to the solution of their private problem that *all* schools should be good, but only that there should be some good school geographically available. But for wage-earning parents nothing suffices except reform in the elementary schools. As one parent will object to the reforms which another parent desires, nothing will serve except an energetic educational propaganda, which is not likely to prove effective until long after the reformer's children are grown up. Thus from love for our own children we are driven, step by step, into the wider sphere of politics and philosophy.

From this wider sphere I desire, in the following pages, to remain aloof as far as possible. The greater part of what I have to say will not be dependent upon the views that I may happen to hold as regards the major controversies of our age. But *complete* independence in this regard is impossible. The education we desire for our children must depend upon our ideals of human character, and our hopes as to the part they are to play in the community. A pacifist will not desire for his children the education which seems good to a militarist; the educational outlook of a communist will not be the same as that of an individualist. To come to a more fundamental cleavage; there can be no agreement between those who regard education as a means of instilling certain definite beliefs, and those who think that it should produce the power of independent judgment. Where such issues are relevant, it would be idle to shirk them. At the same time, there is a considerable body of new knowledge in psychology and pedagogy which is independent of these ultimate questions, and has an intimate bearing on education. Already it has produced very important results, but a great deal remains to be done before its teachings have been fully assimilated. This is especially true of the first five years of life; these have been found to have an importance far greater than that formerly attributed to them, which involves a corresponding increase in the educational importance of parents. . . .

I propose, in what follows, to consider first the aims of education: the kind of individuals, and the kind of community, that we may reasonably hope to see produced by education applied to raw material of the present quality. I ignore the question of the improvement of the breed, whether by eugenics or by any other process, natural or artificial, since this is essentially outside the problems of education. But I attach great weight to modern psychological discoveries which tend to show that character is determined by early education to a much greater extent than was thought by the most enthusiastic educationists of former generations. I distinguish between education of character and education in knowledge, which may be called instruction in the strict sense. The distinction is useful, though not ultimate: some virtues are required in a pupil who is to become instructed, and much knowledge is required for the successful practice of many important virtues. For purposes of discussion, however, instruction can be kept apart from education of character. I shall deal first with education of character, because it is especially important in early years; but I shall carry it through to adolescence, and deal, under this head, with the important question of sex-education. Finally, I shall discuss intellectual education, its aims, its curriculum, and its possibilities, from the first lessons in reading and writing to the end of the university years. The further education which men and women derive from life and the world I shall regard as lying outside my scope; but to make men and women capable of learning from experience should be one of the aims which early education should keep most prominently in view.

BR OE 7–9

What is the true end of education? But before attempting to answer this question it will be well to define the sense in which we are to use the word 'education'. For this purpose I shall distinguish the sense in which I mean to use it from two others, both perfectly legitimate, the one broader and the other narrower than the sense in which I mean to use the word.

In the broader sense, education will include not only what we learn through instruction, but all that we learn through personal experience—the formation of character through the education of life. Of this aspect of education, vitally important as it is, I will say nothing, since its consideration would introduce topics quite foreign to the question with which we are concerned.

In the narrower sense, education may be confined to instruction, the imparting of definite information on various subjects, because such information, in and for itself, is useful in daily life. Elementary education—reading, writing, and arithmetic—is almost wholly of this kind. But instruction, necessary as it is, does not *per se* constitute education in the sense in which I wish to consider it.

Education, in the sense in which I mean it, may be defined as *the formation, by means of instruction, of certain mental habits and a certain outlook on life and the world.* It remains to ask ourselves, what mental habits, and what sort of outlook, can be hoped for as the result of instruction? When we have answered this question we can attempt to decide what science has to contribute to the formation of the habits and outlook which we desire.

BR ML 33

HOW SURROUNDING CONDITIONS KEEP TEACHERS FROM PURSUING THE SOCIAL AIM

The social aim of education, as we have seen, has been a predominant emphasis throughout our national history in all those discussions intended to define and defend the work of public education. But in spite of professed aims and purposes the actual daily work of our schools has in the main given little more than lip service to the social function. It is this failure to live up to professed aims that constitutes the theme of the present chapter. The effort will be to review the factors and conditions which surround the teacher and hinder the realization of the social aims in such a way as to prepare for the fuller discussion of the later chapters.

THE FORMAL TRADITION AND THE SOCIAL AIM

Most obvious among such hindering conditions stands the common tradition, imbedded alike in ordinary school practice and in the expectation of parents, that the work of the school is properly limited to a few simple and formal school subjects, the assigning of lessons in these, and hearing the pupils recite what had been assigned. This type of school practice took shape when the ordinary process of living in the home and community sufficed to give the principal preparation for the simpler life of that day, so that the school need only add 'book learning', and not much of that. In those days the hard conditions of ordinary living combined with the limited outlook and inadequate preparation of teachers to keep the usual school program of the time down to a minimum core of quite formal school subjects. Statesmen and educators might speak nobly of the diffusion of knowledge necessary to successful popular government or of the requisite social and moral virtues, but teachers generally went their way teaching the 3 R's to the younger pupils, adding grammar and locational geography and possibly history as the pupils grew older; while in the secondary school the ancient languages with mathematics and perhaps rhetoric constituted the main reliance. Everywhere, whatever the subjects taught, content and procedure alike followed in the main the same formal and fact-stressing character.

The traditional school was thus a place where lessons were assigned and recited. The verb *recite*, as here used, is highly indicative. To each question asked there was always one and only one right answer. Subject-matter was, on this theory, the kind of thing that could be assigned and then required under penalty. If the assignment were not recited precisely as required, the pupil could be held responsible for his failure and appropriate punishment inflicted. It was on such a conception of the educative process that the graded school was built. A business-like efficiency was sought. When the quota of subject-matter set out for the first year (or grade) had been so learned that it could be given back on demand, then the pupil was promoted to the second year. Otherwise he must repeat the grade. The curriculum was the stated succession of annual quotas of subject-matter thus set out to be learned. Report cards indicated relative progress in quota achievement. Honor rolls were introduced to foster competitive effort. Supervision, following the further example of business efficiency, existed to see that teachers properly exacted the prescribed quotas and otherwise attended to their duties.

On this traditional basis the social aim, if considered at all, was supposedly cared for in history and civics, each taught—typically so, at least—on the same formal and factual basis already noted. The history was so written as to show that our country has always been right in whatever it has done, while the civics gave the structural explanation of such uniform excellence. That the school could concern itself with the social understandings of pupils or with the problems of society about them was beyond conception. With such a content and with the prevailing procedure, seldom or never was there opportunity to raise questions or consider problems of current interest. As long as the teaching method was based explicitly on one and only one right answer, and that known in advance to the teacher and (except perhaps in mathematics) also to the pupil, there could hardly be a discussion of unsettled issues. Such an education tended by its essential processes to be indoctrination. What was taught was taught on authority, and the pupils were expected to accept it on authority.

That these traditions still exist, not in 100 per cent degree to be sure but still in strength, cannot be seriously questioned. By them as standards do many parents still tend to judge the school their children attend. School boards, and laymen in general, tend to think in these terms. Proposed innovations that would alter this tradition meet curiously stubborn opposition. When depression comes and tax-reduction leagues infest the land, little difficulty is experienced in cutting out as 'fads and thrills' anything and everything that does not conform to this tradition.

WHK TS 26–8

The kernel of the scientific outlook is a thing so simple, so obvious, so seemingly trivial, that the mention of it may almost excite derision. The kernel of the scientific outlook is the refusal to regard our own desires, tastes and interests as affording a key to the understanding of the world. Stated thus baldly, this may seem no more than a trite truism. But to remember it consistently in matters arousing our passionate partisanship is by no means easy, especially where the available evidence is uncertain and inconclusive. A few illustrations will make this clear....

We may take as another illustration Malthus's doctrine of population. This illustration is all the better for the fact that his actual doctrine is now known to be largely erroneous. It is not his conclusions that are valuable, but the temper and method of his inquiry. As everyone knows, it was to him that Darwin owed an essential part of his theory of natural selection, and this was only possible because Malthus's outlook was truly scientific. His great merit lies in considering man not as the object of praise or blame, but as a part of nature, a thing with a certain characteristic behaviour from which certain consequences must follow. If the behaviour it not quite what Malthus supposed, if the consequences are not quite what he inferred, that may falsify his conclusions, but does not impair the value of his method. The objections which were made when his doctrine was new—that it was horrible and depressing, that people ought not to act as he said they did, and so on—were all such as implied an unscientific attitude of mind; as against all of them, his calm determination to treat man as a natural phenomenon marks an important advance over the reformers of the eighteenth century and the Revolution.

Under the influence of Darwinism the scientific attitude towards man has now become fairly common, and is to some people quite natural, though to most it it is still a difficult and artificial contortion. There is, however, one study which is as yet almost wholly untouched by the scientific spirit—I mean the study of philosophy. . . .

Now in philosophy this attitude of mind has not as yet been achieved. A certain self-absorption, not personal, but human, has marked almost all attempts to conceive the universe as a whole. Mind, or some aspect of it—thought or will or sentience—has been regarded as the pattern after which the universe is to be conceived, for no better reason, at bottom, than that such a universe would not seem strange, and would give us the cosy feeling that every place is like home. To conceive the universe as essentially progressive or essentially deteriorating, for example, is to give to our hopes and fears a cosmic importance which *may*, of course, be justified, but which we have as yet no reason to suppose justified. Until we have learnt to think of it in ethically neutral terms, we have not arrived at a scientific attitude in philosophy; and until we have arrived at such an attitude, it is hardly to be hoped that philosophy will achieve any solid results.

I have spoken so far largely of the negative aspect of the scientific spirit, but it is from the positive aspect that its value is derived. The instinct of constructiveness, which is one of the chief incentives to artistic creation, can find in scientific systems a satisfaction more massive than any epic poem. Disinterested curiosity, which is the source of almost all intellectual effort, finds with astonished delight that science can unveil secrets which might well have seemed for ever undiscoverable. The desire for a larger life and wider interests, for an escape from private circumstances, and even from the whole recurring human cycle of birth and death, is fulfilled by the impersonal cosmic outlook of science as by nothing else. To all these must be added, as contributing to the happiness of the man of science, the admiration of splendid achievement, and the consciousness of inestimable utility to the human race. A life devoted to science is therefore a happy life, and its happiness is derived from the very best sources that are open to dwellers on this troubled and passionate planet.

BR ML 37–9

'That's nothing but common sense, isn't it? Where does the science come in?'

'Science is itself nothing but common sense, common sense more careful of its steps. Science is based on experience just as common sense is, but it has more exact ways of measuring and of telling. In particular it tries to include many experiences under one statement. A law of nature is merely a very inclusive, very careful, and very reliable statement of what to expect.'

'That sounds reasonable, but apply it to our topic. What is a law of learning?'

'A law of learning would be nothing but a very carefully made and very inclusive statement of how learning takes place.'

'Give us one of the laws of learning. I'd like to know how learning takes place. Perhaps I'd know better how to make my pupils learn.'

'I'll give you the Law of Readiness: When a bond is ready to act, to act gives satisfaction and not to act—'

'Now there you go again with your outlandish jargon. Why don't you use everyday English.'

WHK FM 21

THE CONTRIBUTION OF BIOLOGY TO UNDERSTANDING OF THE LIFE PROCESS

We saw above a brief analysis of the behaviour process, with its emphasis on the organism and its responding to a stirring situation. We wish now to see more in detail how biology can help to an understanding of the life process.

Prior to Darwin no discussion of the human individual in relation to the course of life would have begun in this biological fashion. Some, following Aristotelian logic, would have stressed the intellect as man's peculiar endowment, probably speaking of man as *Homo sapiens*. Others, following a widespread interest of the time, would have stressed the 'fallen nature' of man, his consequent sinfulness, and punishment visited on him in the way of sickness, plant pests, and the like. Still others, more modern, would have followed Adam Smith and Jeremy Bentham in stressing the opportunity of self-seeking individuals to prosper under a regime of freedom.

But now we start the study of life and of philosophy with the behaving process and see behavior as life itself in action. We find that, while behavior differs from one animal species to another, there are none the less many features in common. Of the eight terms listed below as helpful in the biologic approach to human life and behavior only one, thinking in its fuller sense, is limited to man. However, the descriptions as given best fit man and are so intended; for it is man and his behavior that concern us in this book.

Consider now in detail the following biological conceptions which were either explicitly or implicitly given just above:

Organism—a living being organized for carrying on life; here a person (technically, an 'agent') stirred to action.

Behavior—the effort at control, all that the organism does, inside and out, in response to the stirring; all the thoughts, feelings, physical movements (inside and out) called into play by the disturbing or arousing situation; specifically, all that the organism does to control the situation in order to care for the values felt to be involved or at stake.

The environment—everything, apart from the organism, that affects, either directly or indirectly, the behavior of the organism, including many things of which the organism consciously knows little or nothing.

The situation—this is, in each case of action, the environment-as-the-organism-'sees'-it, including the possible means of action; the 'situation' as thus defined will change somewhat as the experience develops.

Goal-seeking—the act and fact of setting up aims and pursuing them; the fact that the agent sees values so involved in the situation as to stir him to defined action in pursuit of them.

Preferences—the crucial factor in any stirring. There would be no response if the organism had no preferences as to what may happen to him, no preferences waiting to be stirred to action by a situation capable of stirring hopes or fears.

Feeling—that aspect of behaving which has to do with pleasure or pain, with satisfaction or dissatisfaction. Normally, feeling or emotion serves as an organic resource to heighten action. Glow of interest and anticipation causes the organism to strive harder and at the same time adds enjoyment to the process. Emotion may, however, as in anger, for example, so overdo the heightening as to bring later regrets.

WHK PE 19-20

The love of knowledge to which the growth of science is due is itself the product of a twofold impulse. We may seek knowledge of an object because we love the object or because we wish to have power over it. The former impulse leads to the kind of knowledge that is contemplative, the latter to the kind that is practical. In the development of science the power impulse has increasingly prevailed over the love impulse. The power impulse is embodied in industrialism and in governmental technique. It is embodied also in the philosophies known as pragmatism and instrumentalism. Each of these philosophies holds, broadly speaking, that our beliefs about any object are true in so far as they enable us to manipulate it with advantage to ourselves. This is what may be called a governmental view of truth. Of truth so conceived science offers us a great deal; indeed there seems no limit to its possible triumphs. To the man who wishes to change his environment science offers astonishingly powerful tools, and if knowledge consists in the power to produce intended changes, then science gives knowledge in abundance.

But the desire for knowledge has another form, belonging to an entirely different set of emotions. The mystic, the lover, and the poet are also seekers after knowledge—not perhaps very successful seekers, but none the less worthy of respect on that account. In all forms of love we wish to have knowledge of what is loved, not for purposes of power, but for the ecstasy of contemplation. 'In knowledge of God standeth our eternal life,' but not because knowledge of God gives us power over Him. Wherever there is ecstasy or joy or delight derived from an object there is the desire to know that object—to know it not in the manipulative fashion that consists of turning it into something else, but to know it in the fashion of the beatific vision, because in itself and for itself it sheds happiness upon the lover. In sex love as in other forms of love this impulse to this kind of knowledge exists, unless the love is purely physical or practical. This may indeed be made the touchstone of any love that is valuable. Love which has value contains an impulse towards that kind of knowledge out of which the mystic union springs.

Science in its beginnings was due to men who were in love with the world. They perceived the beauty of the stars and the sea, of the winds and the mountains. Because they loved them their thoughts dwelt upon them, and they wished to understand them more intimately than a mere outward contemplation made possible.

'The world,' said Heraclitus, 'is an ever-living fire, with measures kindling and measures going out.' Heraclitus and the other Ionian philosophers, from whom came the first impulse to scientific knowledge, felt the strange beauty of the world almost like a madness in the blood. They were men of Titanic passionate intellect, and from the intensity of their intellectual passion the whole movement of the modern world has sprung. But step by step, as science has developed, the impulse of love which gave it birth has been increasingly thwarted, while the impulse of power, which was at first a mere camp-follower, has gradually usurped command in virtue of its unforeseen success. The lover of nature has been baffled, the tyrant over nature has been rewarded. As physics has developed, it has deprived us step by step of what we thought we knew concerning the intimate nature of the physical world. Colour and sound, light and shade, form and texture, belong no longer to that external nature that the Ionians sought as the bride of their devotion.

BR SO 270–2

When I come to die I shall not feel that I have lived in vain. I have seen the earth turn red at evening, the dew sparkling in the morning, and the snow shining under a frosty sun; I have smelt rain after drought, and have heard the stormy Atlantic beat upon the granite shores of Cornwall. Science may bestow these and other joys upon more people than could otherwise enjoy them. If so, its power will be wisely used. But when it takes out of life the moments to which life owes its value, science will not deserve admiration, however cleverly and however elaborately it may lead men along the road to despair. The sphere of values lies outside science, except in so far as science consists in the pursuit of knowledge. Science as the pursuit of power must not obtrude upon the sphere of values, and scientific technique, if it is to enrich human life, must not outweigh the ends which it should serve.

BR SO 275

'Come over to the States,' he said with eagerness; 'we want men of your ideas over there. I reckon that you and the new schools there don't differ at all.'

I gave him my impressions of the American schools described by Dewey in his book.

'It seems to me,' I said, 'that these schools over-emphasize the "learn by doing" business. Almost every modern reformer in education talks of "child processes"; the kindergarten idea is carried all the way. Children are encouraged to shape things with their hands.'

'Sure,' he said, 'but that's only a preliminary to shaping things with their heads.'

'I'm not so sure that the one naturally leads to the other,' I went on. 'Learning by doing is a fine thing, but when little Willie asks why rabbits have white tails the learning by doing business breaks down. In America you have workshops where boys mould metal; you have school farms. But I hold that a child can have all that for years and yet be badly educated.'

He looked amazed.

'But I thought that was your line,' he said with puzzled expression, 'Montessori, and all that kind of thing!'

'I don't know what Montessorianism is,' I said; 'I have forgotten everything I ever read about Froebel and Pestalozzi. All I know is that reformers want the child to follow its own processes—whatever that phrase may mean. I heartily agree with them when they say that the child should choose its own line, and should discover knowledge for itself. But my point is that a boy may act every incident in history, for instance, and never realize what history means. I can't see the educational value of children acting the incident of Alfred and the burnt cakes.'

'Ah! but isn't self-expression a great thing?'

'It is,' I answered, 'but the actor doesn't express himself. Irving expressed himself . . and the result was that Shakespeare was Irvingized. A school pageant of the accession of Henry IV may be a fine spectacle, but it is emphasizing all the stuff that doesn't matter a damn in history.'

'But,' he protested, 'it is the stuff that matters to children. You forget that a child isn't a little adult.'

'This brings us to the vexed question of the coming in of the adult,' I said. 'You and I agree that the adult should interfere as little as possible; but the adult will come in in spite of us. Leave children to themselves and they express their personalities the live-long day. Every game is an expression of individuality. The adult steps in and says "We must guide these children," and he takes their attention from playing houses to playing scenes from history. And I want to know the educational value of it all.'

'It is like travel,' he said. 'When you travel places become real to you, and when you travel back into mediæval times the whole thing becomes real to you.'

'I see your point,' I said, 'and in a manner I agree with you. But why select pageants? You will agree with me when I say that the condition of the people in feudal times is of far greater importance than the display of a Henry.'

'Certainly, I do.'

'And the things of real importance in history are incapable of being dramatized. You can make a modern school act the Signing of Magna Charta, but the children won't understand the meaning of Magna Charta any the better. You can't dramatize the Enclosure of the Public Lands in Tudor Times; you can't dramatize the John Ball insurrection; all the acting in the world won't help you to understand the Puritan Revolution.'

'You are thinking of children as little adults,' he said.

'But they *are* little adults! Every game is an imitation of adult processes; the ring games down at the school there nearly all deal with love and matrimony; the girls make houses and take in lodgers. And if you persuade them to act the part of King Alfred you are encouraging them to be little adults. They are children when they cry and run and jump; whenever they reason they reason as adults. They are very often in the company of adults . . . and that's one of the reasons why you cannot trust what are called child processes. . . .

'If the children had not been going to homes at night I should have trusted to freedom alone. As it was the poor bairns were between two fires. I gave them freedom . . . and their parents cursed me. One woman sent a verbal message to me to the effect that I was an idiot; one bright little lassie came to me one day with the words of the woman next door, "It's just waste o' time attendin' that schule." Do you imagine that all the child processes in the world could save a child from an environment like that?'

When the American departed he held out his hand.

'I came to see a reformer of child education,' he said with a smile, and I discover that you aren't a reformer of child education at all; your job in life is to run a school for parents.'

ASN DD 103–7

Belief and propaganda

The habit of teaching some one orthodoxy, political, religious, or moral, has all kinds of bad effects. To begin with, it excludes from the teaching profession men who combine honesty with intellectual vigour, who are just the men likely to have the best moral and mental effect upon their pupils. I will give three illustrations. First, as to politics: a teacher of economics in America is expected to teach such doctrines as will add to the wealth and power of the very rich; if he does not, he finds it advisable to go elsewhere.... Second, as to religion: the immense majority of intellectually eminent men disbelieve the Christian religion, but they conceal the fact in public, because they are afraid of losing their incomes. Thus on the most important of all subjects most of the men whose opinions and arguments would be best worth having are condemned to silence. Third, as to morals: Practically all men are unchaste at some time of their lives; clearly those who conceal this fact are worse than those who do not, since they add the guilt of hypocrisy. But it is only to the hypocrites that teaching posts are open. So much for the effects of orthodoxy upon the choice and character of teachers.

I come now to the effect upon the pupils, which I will take under two heads, intellectual and moral. Intellectually, what is stimulating to a young man is a problem of obvious practical importance, as to which he finds that divergent opinions are held. A young man learning economics, for example, ought to hear lectures from individualists and socialists, protectionists and free-traders, inflationists and believers in the gold standard. He ought to be encouraged to read the best books of the various schools, as recommended by those who believe in them. This would teach him to weigh arguments and evidence, to know that no opinion is certainly right, and to judge men by their quality rather than by their consonance with preconceptions. History should be taught not only from the point of view of one's own country, but also from that of foreigners. If history were taught by Frenchmen in England, and by Englishmen in France, there would be no disagreements between the two countries, because each would understand the other's point of view. A young man should learn to think that all questions are open, and that an argument should be followed wherever it leads. The needs of practical life will destroy this attitude all too soon when he begins to earn his living; but until that time he should be encouraged to taste the joys of free speculation. . . .

When a school accepts as part of its task the teaching of an opinion which cannot be intellectually defended (as practically all schools do), it is compelled to give the impression that those who hold an opposite opinion are wicked, since otherwise it cannot generate the passion required for repelling the assaults of reason. Thus for the sake of orthodoxy the children are rendered uncharitable, intolerant, cruel, and bellicose. This is unavoidable so long as definite opinions are prescribed on politics, morals, and religion.

BR SE 198–200

Another reason why I am not wholly on the side of Montessori is, I fancy, that her religious attitude repels me. She is a church woman; she has a definite idea of right and wrong. Thus, although she allows children freedom to choose their own occupations, she allows them no freedom to challenge adult morality. But for a child to accept a ready-made code of morals is dangerous; education in morality is a thousand times more important than intellectual education with a didactic apparatus.

ASN DD 148

EDUCATION *VS.* INDOCTRINATION

The education thus far discussed is an education designed to free the whole personality of the learner for the fullest living, for the best and most independent exercise of all his powers, for the control of his own destiny. This alone we have counted true respect for the personality. It was further brought out that without such development the individual is not free in perhaps the most important sense, that true and effective freedom depends thus as much on inner growth, on the ability to use the mind effectively, as on the absence of external restraint. In fact, it might be said that a condition of inner slavery is the worst kind of slavery; such an individual has no wish to change his status, he even fights against his true freedom. To aid the individual, then, to the fullest use of his powers, to fullest intelligent and responsible self-direction and effectiveness, is to give the greatest possible respect to his personality.

But teachers have not always thus sought to respect the personalities of those studying under them; many today still act otherwise. In other words, teachers have too often cared more for the subject-matter they teach or the cause they represent than for human personality. In the early days of the Protestant Revolt, for example, both sides alike competed for proselytes, each side struggling to get control of as many youth as they could in the effort to fasten their respective doctrines upon the minds and hearts of the young under their care. It was only at a later date, under the democratic teaching of respect for personality, that men grew to the point of questioning such partisan indoctrination.

The term *indoctrination* just used demands a word of explanation. The word means, literally, implanting doctrines. When such implanting on an uncritical basis was the common practice of the school, and indeed one of its principal aims, to indoctrinate and to teach came to be but diverse ways of describing the same process. The term *indoctrination* then carried no derogatory implication, and this was until recently its recognized meaning and status. The Oxford English Dictionary (this part published about 1900) recognized no other meaning. But with the development of democracy and the coming of modern rapid change, it was increasingly felt that education could no longer be content with inducing uncritical belief, but must instead develop responsible thinking on the part of all as a necessary preparation for democratic living and citizenship and an unpredictable future. In this way the term *indoctrination* has been increasingly restricted to its derogatory implication of an improper inducing of uncritical belief.

There are, to be sure, some who still believe it right for parents and teachers to implant their own doctrines in the young under their care so that these doctrines will remain fixed beyond the possibility of later question or revision. These people accordingly use the term *indoctrination* with a favorable implication. Also, curiously enough, during the late war the American Navy adapted the term *indoctrination* to mean 'instruction in the fundamentals of military discipline, naval customs, and usage.' Naturally this interpretation carries no derogatory implication. And this naval use of the term has since been extended to other areas. So that the term is currently used in several different senses, the one here followed being, however, the more usual meaning in educational writing.

That democracy must refuse and reject indoctrination in this prejudice-building sense would seem beyond question. Where competent opinion differs as to what to believe, for parents and teachers to take advantage of the child's ignorance and docility to fasten in him beyond recall their own chosen views is to enslave this child to those who thus teach him. Democracy and a proper respect for the child's personality must reject such enslavement as partisan exploitation of the individual's right to be educated to do his own thinking and make his own decisions....

3. While agreeing that indoctrination in other matters is wrong, some still feel that the case for democracy is different; for it we should indoctrinate. They claim (i) that, democracy being fundamental to our way of living, we should run no risk regarding it, but indoctrinate all in it from earliest childhood. They point further to the facts (ii) that our democracy is now threatened from without as never before and (iii), sad to say, that some of our own people do not even now fully accept democracy. From these considerations, they say, indoctrination of all is demanded.

To such a proposal the reply seems to be to agree to the three facts and assert that the conclusion does not follow. To teach democracy in undemocratic fashion, in a way to foster uncritical acceptance, would seem an odd way of fostering democracy. To indoctrinate a belief in democracy without including the reasons for democracy, and without building ability to think critically about it, is to make blindfolded adherents of democracy. Such people would not know the why of their practices or dogmas and consequently could not be trusted to apply the doctrines intelligently. When they grow up into active citizenship they might be easily induced, for example, to forbid the study of controversial issues in school. They might forbid the critical study of democratic doctrines and so prevent wise adaptation of these doctrines to new conditions that arise. In one word, such indoctrination would make blind dogmatists of democracy, quite unfit to carry on the democratic process in a changing civilization. That way lies fanaticism.

The conclusion of the whole matter, it appears, is that democracy and ethics must at bottom respect the personality of all concerned, to develop each as best possible toward more effective use of his mind and toward intelligent and responsible free play of intelligence. On this we must stand. Such respect for personality is indeed the most sacred thing among men.

WHK PE 121–3, 125

PROPAGANDA

In my school I have never attempted to get children to share my beliefs or my prejudices. . . .

I have no religion but have never taught one word against religion, nor against the barbarous criminal code, nor anti-Semitism, nor imperialism. I have never influenced children to become pacifists or vegetarians or temperance reformers. My propaganda is a subtle one; I know that preaching cuts no ice with children, so I put my trust in the power of freedom to fortify youth against sham and fanaticism and isms of any kind. Yes, I leave freedom to counteract organized propaganda for what, to me, are evil things . . . not meaning that pacifism and vegetarianism, etc. are evil of course. But when my daughter of six came to me and said: 'Willie has the biggest cock among the small kids, but Mrs X (a visitor) says it is rude to say cock,' I at once told her volubly that it was not rude, and inwardly cursed the woman for her ignorant and narrow understanding of children. I might tolerate propaganda from other people about politics or manners, but when anyone attacks my own child or any other child, making it guilty about sex, I bring all my batteries into action and fight back vigorously. Put it this way: propaganda for—say—a political theory may and will affect the child emotionally, but propaganda by Mrs Grundy goes straight to the solar plexus. A child can grow out of being a Labourite or a Tory or a Communist, but the life-hating prejudices of a sex obsessionist are likely to open up the way to a neurotic adulthood. Politics may start in the emotions but in the end the intellect comes into play; with a Mrs Grundy repression the intellect cannot influence what is fixed firmly in the solar plexus.

The advocates of propaganda say something like this: There is a vast amount of subtle propaganda that must affect the children—the pornographic laugh in the cinema, the hush-hush about birth, the press with its reports of crimes, the news reels with their glorification of tanks and bombs, the magistrates with their moral lectures. Is it fair to children to let the devil play them all the worst tunes? I answer cheerfully that if you preserve your child from guilt, especially guilt about its body and its sex, it will come almost unscathed through the most dangerous barrage of moral and sinister big guns. I say *almost* unscathed and that 'almost' is what makes me keep a sharp eye on the Grundy woman.

ASN FC 124–5

Character and moral education

Then he brought forward the old argument that freedom like that was handicapping them for after life; they would not face difficulties.

'Hugh was up against a greater difficulty than most boys ever come up against,' I said, 'and he faced it bravely and confidently. When you are free from authority you have a will of your own; you know exactly what you want and you set your teeth and get it. You are on your own, you have acquired responsibility. Given a dictating teacher or parent a boy will do the minimum on his own responsibility. Good lord! if I make all these youngsters sit up and attend strenuously to my speaking I am not training them to face difficulties; I am simply bullying them, making them a subject race.'

'You are training character.'

'I would be training children to obey, and the first thing a child should learn is to be a rebel. If a man isn't a rebel by the time he is twenty-five, God help him! Character simply means a man's nature, and I refuse to change a man's nature by force; I leave the experiment to the judges and prison warders.'

I want to ask every dominie who believes in coercion what he thinks of the results of many years' coercion. Obviously present-day civilization with its criminal division of humanity into parasites and slaves is all wrong.

'But,' a dominie might cry, 'can you definitely blame elementary education for that?'

I answer: 'Yes, yes, yes!'

The manhood of Britain today has passed through the schools; they have been lulled to sleep; they have never learned to face the awful truth about civilization. And I blame the coercion of the teachers. Train a boy to obey his teacher and he will naturally obey every dirty politician who has the faculty of rhetoric; he will naturally believe the lies of every dirty newspaper proprietor that is playing his own dirty game.

ASN DD 64–6

A person's character is the organized aggregate of his tendencies to behavior—specifically, his tendencies to regular and predictable behavior. In the degree, then, that one has character he will tend to behave—think, feel, choose, act—in accordance with the personality patterns he has accumulated (learned) through the years. We thus say of a certain person that kindliness or considerateness is 'characteristic' of him. If we then hear that this person has acted harshly, we say that is 'not like him.'

To appraise one's character in this way indicates the assumption, suggested in the opening sentence, that a character is an organized, interactive whole. And this seems demonstrably true. All parts and aspects of a well-built character do cooperate in the service of its accepted underlying principles of action. This action as a whole gives, as we saw earlier, efficacy to the act; but, with principles also involved, it does more than that, it gives *appropriateness of action,* appropriateness to fit the principles of action previously organized into the character.

Thus in each act there are involved all of one's habits, dispositions, and tendencies, each according to the degree of its pertinence to the matter at hand. Each one accordingly feels as it is 'like him' to feel, including of course his peculiar impulsiveness and 'aberrations'; he thinks out of his own specific insight and understanding; he acts morally according to what he accepts as right to do; his motor habits come into action in accordance with their previously organized connection with his feelings and thoughts. This is character in operation.

It is, then, the internally organized aggregate of all one's habits —insights, dispositions, any psychological tendencies—which constitute his character, which make him what he is as an individual. *The Oxford English Dictionary* defines character as 'the aggregate of the distinctive features of anything,' 'the sum of the moral and mental qualities which distinguish an individual.' Each real character is thus necessarily unique. It is the fact of the interpenetration of habits (taking habit in its broad sense) which makes character possible, the fact that all work together and that each affects the others. In fact John Dewey says that 'character is the interpenetration of habits,' having just asserted that 'were it not for the continued operation of all habits in every act, no such thing as character could exist.' (46:38) To say that 'all habits' thus operate 'in every act' may appear a bit strong; but when we consider how habits do act, the assertion seems justified. It is out of this fact that we can have regularized, predictable behavior.

It should not be misunderstood from the foregoing discussion that character alone is the sole source of behavior; the environment is also a true factor, as we shall later consider in some detail. In a true sense, character and environment are, so to say, mother and father of behavior. That is, character is, as indicated, the psychological structure which sums up in one organic whole all of the individual's prior experiences, and out of which, in its interaction with the environment, behavior emerges.

Character is, as we saw above, regularized. It may of course be regularly bad as truly as regularly good. However, in the more usual sense, a man of character is a man with tendencies toward worthy behavior. Webster's *Dictionary of Synonyms* gives the quotation: 'When we say of such and such a man that he has . . . character, we generally mean that he has disciplined his temperament, his disposition, into strict obedience to the behests of duty.' Bertrand Russell speaks to the same effect of the achieved 'power of pursuing a distant object steadily, foregoing and suffering many things on the way. This involves the subordination of impulse to will, the power of directing action by large desires even at moments when they are not vividly alive. Without this, no serious ambition, good or bad, can be realized, no consistent purpose can dominate.' (143:170f.)

What is the relation of character and personality? Are the two identical? Or do they need to be distinguished? Character is the inclusive term which takes in all aspects of the organism's behavior in relation to itself and its environment; it is the habit aspect of the whole, recognizing that habits are not merely motor or physical, but mental and emotional as well. In other words, as indicated earlier, character means the sum of all one's tendencies to regularized and predictable behavior, which includes the personality.

Personality is an aspect of character, and accordingly is distinguishable from character. Personality is the self-conscious, self-directing self. Though the term is less inclusive, personality is the central and crucial essence of character, the self as it feels and thinks about itself, about others, about things, about values, all in terms of the interrelations of the person with his environment.

Thus any discussion of character necessarily includes personality. But certain aspects of personality-building require special treatment and will therefore be discussed in a separate chapter. Here will be discussed the building of the character and the desirable content to be built into character.

WHK PE 356–8

I will take four characteristics which seem to me jointly to form the basis of an ideal character; vitality, courage, sensitiveness, and intelligence. I do not suggest that this list is complete, but I think it carries us a good way. Moreover, I firmly believe that, by proper physical, emotional, and intellectual care of the young, these qualities could all be made very common. I shall consider each in turn.

Vitality is rather a physiological than a mental characteristic; it is presumably always present where there is perfect health, but it tends to ebb with advancing years, and gradually dwindles to nothing in old age. In vigorous children it quickly rises to a maximum before they reach school age, and then tends to be diminished by education. Where it exists, there is pleasure in feeling alive, quite apart from any specific pleasant circumstances. It heightens pleasures and diminishes pains. It makes it easy to take an interest in whatever occurs, and thus promotes objectivity, which is an essential of sanity. Human beings are prone to become absorbed in themselves, unable to be interested in what they see and hear or in anything outside their own skins. This is a great misfortune to themselves, since it entails at best boredom and at worst melancholia; it is also a fatal barrier to usefulness, except in very exceptional cases. Vitality promotes interest in the outside world; it also promotes the power of hard work. Moreover, it is a safeguard against envy, because it makes one's own existence pleasant. As envy is one of the great sources of human misery, this is a very important merit in vitality. Many bad qualities are of course compatible with vitality—for example, those of a healthy tiger. And many of the best qualities are compatible with its absence: Newton and Locke, for example, had very little. Both these men, however, had irritabilities and envies from which better health would have set them free....

Courage—the second quality on our list—has several forms, and all of them are complex. Absence of fear is one thing, and the power of controlling fear is another. And absence of fear, in turn, is one thing when the fear is rational, another when it is irrational. Absence of irrational fear is clearly good; so is the power of controlling fear. But absence of rational fear is a matter as to which debate is possible. However, I shall postpone this question until I have said something about the other forms of courage.

Sensitiveness, the third quality in our list, is in a sense a corrective of mere courage. Courageous behaviour is easier for a man who fails to apprehend dangers, but such courage may often be foolish. We cannot regard as satisfactory any way of acting which is dependent upon ignorance or forgetfulness: the fullest possible knowledge and realization are an essential part of what is desirable. The cognitive aspect, however, comes under the head of intelligence; sensitiveness, in the sense in which I am using the term, belongs to the emotions. A purely theoretical definition would be that a person is emotionally sensitive when many stimuli produce emotions in him; but taken thus broadly the quality is not necessarily a good one. If sensitiveness is to be good, the emotional reaction must be in some sense *appropriate*: mere intensity is not what is needed. The quality I have in mind is that of being affected pleasurably or the reverse by many things, and by the right things. What are the right things, I shall try to explain.

Cognitive sensitiveness, which should also be included, is practically the same thing as a habit of observation, and this is more naturally considered in connection with intelligence. Aesthetic sensitiveness raises a number of problems which I do not wish to discuss at this stage. I will therefore pass on to the last of the four qualities we enumerated, namely, intelligence.

One of the great defects of traditional morality has been the low estimate it placed upon intelligence. The Greeks did not err in this respect, but the Church led men to think that nothing matters except virtue, and virtue consists in abstinence from a certain list of actions arbitrarily labelled 'sin'. So long as this attitude persists, it is impossible to make men realize that intelligence does more good than an artificial conventional 'virtue'. When I speak of intelligence, I include both actual knowledge and receptivity to knowledge. The two are, in fact, closely connected. Ignorant adults are unteachable; on such matters as hygiene or diet, for example, they are totally incapable of believing what science has to say. The more a man has learnt, the easier it is for him to learn still more—always assuming that he has not been taught in a spirit of dogmatism. Ignorant people have never been compelled to change their mental habits, and have stiffened into an unchangeable attitude. It is not only that they are credulous where they should be sceptical; it is just as much that they are incredulous where they should be receptive. No doubt the word 'intelligence' properly signifies rather an aptitude for acquiring knowledge than knowledge already acquired; but I do not think this aptitude is acquired except by exercise, any more than the aptitude of a pianist or an acrobat. It is, of course, possible to impart information in ways that do not train intelligence; it is not only possible, but easy, and frequently done. But I do not believe that it is possible to train intelligence without imparting information, or at any rate causing knowledge to be acquired. And without intelligence our complex modern world cannot subsist; still less can it make progress. I regard the cultivation of intelligence, therefore, as one of the major purposes of education. This might seem a commonplace, but in fact it is not. The desire to instil what are regarded as correct beliefs has made educationists too often indifferent to the training of intelligence. To make this clear, it is necessary to define intelligence a little more closely, so as to discover the mental habits which it requires. For this purpose I shall consider only the aptitude for acquiring knowledge, not the store of actual knowledge which might legitimately be included in the definition of intelligence.

The instinctive foundation of the intellectual life is curiosity, which is found among animals in its elementary forms. Intelligence demands an alert curiosity, but it must be of a certain kind. The sort that leads village neighbours to try to peer through curtains after dark has no very high value. The widespread interest in gossip is inspired, not by a love of knowledge, but by malice: no one gossips about other people's secret virtues, but only about their secret vices. Accordingly most gossip is untrue, but care is taken not to verify it. Our neighbour's sins, like the consolations of religion, are so agreeable that we do not stop to scrutinize the evidence closely. Curiosity properly so-called, on the other hand, is inspired by a genuine love of knowledge. You may see this impulse in a moderately pure form, at work in a cat which has been brought to a strange room, and proceeds to smell every corner and every piece of furniture. You will see it also in children, who are passionately interested when a drawer or cupboard, usually closed, is open for their inspection. Animals, machines, thunderstorms, and all forms of manual work, arouse the curiosity of children, whose thirst for knowledge puts the most intelligent adults to shame. This impulse grows weaker with advancing years, until at last what is unfamiliar inspires only disgust, with no desire for a closer acquaintance. This is the stage at which people announce that the country is going to the dogs, and that 'things are not what they were in my young days'. The thing which is not the same as it was in that far-off time is the speaker's curiosity. And with the death of curiosity we may reckon that active intelligence, also, has died.

But although curiosity lessens in intensity and in extent after childhood, it may for a long time improve in quality. Curiosity about general propositions shows a higher level of intelligence than curiosity about particular facts; broadly speaking, the higher the order of generality, the greater is the intelligence involved. (This rule, however, must not be taken too strictly.) Curiosity dissociated from personal advantage shows a higher development than curiosity connected (say) with a chance of food. The cat that sniffs in a new room is not a wholly disinterested scientific inquirer, but probably also wants to find out whether there are mice about. Perhaps it is not quite correct to say that curiosity is best when it is disinterested, but rather that it is best when the connection with other interests is not direct and obvious, but discoverable only by means of a certain degree of intelligence. This point, however, it is not necessary for us to decide.

If curiosity is to be fruitful, it must be associated with a certain technique for the acquisition of knowledge. There must be habits of observation, belief in the possibility of knowledge, patience, and industry. These things will develop themselves, given the original fund of curiosity and the proper intellectual education. But since our intellectual life is only a part of our activity, and since curiosity is perpetually coming into conflict with other passions, there is need of certain intellectual virtues, such as open-mindedness. We become impervious to new truth both from habit and from desire; we find it hard to disbelieve what we have emphatically believed for a number of years, and also what ministers to self-esteem or any other fundamental passion. Open-mindedness should therefore be one of the qualities that education aims at producing.

BR OE 35–6, 39, 41–3

There is no case whatever for the moral instruction of children. It is psychologically wrong. To ask a little child to be unselfish is wrong. Every child is an egoist. The world belongs to him. His power of wishing is strong; he has only to wish and he is king of the earth. When he has an apple his one wish is to eat that apple. And the chief result of mother's encouraging him to share it with his little brother is to make him hate the little brother. Altruism comes later, comes naturally if the child is not taught to be unselfish; probably never comes at all when the child is taught to be unselfish. Altruism is selfishness on promotion. The altruist is merely the man who likes to please others while he is satisfying his own selfishness.

By suppressing the child's selfishness the mother is fixing that selfishness. An unfulfilled wish lives on in the unconscious. The child who is taught to be unselfish will remain selfish through life. Moral instruction thus defeats its own purpose.

ASN PC 18

The elimination of thoughtless cruelty is to be effected most easily by developing an interest in construction and growth. Almost every child, as soon as he is old enough, wants to kill flies and other insects; this leads on to the killing of larger animals, and ultimately of men. In the ordinary English upper-class family, the killing of birds is considered highly creditable, and the killing of men in war is regarded as the noblest of professions. This attitude is in accordance with untrained instinct: it is that of men who possess no form of constructive skill, and are therefore unable to find any innocent embodiment of their will to power. They can make pheasants die and tenants suffer; when occasion arises, they can shoot a rhinoceros or a German. But in more useful arts they are entirely deficient, as their parents and teachers thought it sufficient to make them into English gentlemen. I do not believe that at birth they are any stupider than other babies;

their deficiencies in later life are entirely attributable to bad education. If, from an early age, they had been led to feel the value of life by watching its development with affectionate proprietorship; if they had acquired forms of constructive skill; if they had been made to realize with apprehension how quickly and easily a slow product of anxious solicitude can be destroyed—if all this had formed part of their early moral training, they would not be so ready to destroy what others have similarly created or tended. The great educator in this respect in later life is parenthood, provided the instinct is adequately aroused. But in the rich this seldom happens, because they leave the care of their children to paid professionals; therefore we cannot wait till they become parents before beginning to eradicate their destructive tendencies.

BR OE 77

When a child has so far developed that he can not only do various things, but knows that he can do them, he then can, we say, *act intentionally*. He can mean to do what he does and know it. He is now ready for the next advance, to understand that these acts of his are part of the public world in which he and others live together. And, accordingly, his elders begin to tell him that he *must not* do this and he *must* do that. In other words they are beginning to hold him *accountable* for what he does, accountable for his conscious and intentional acts. When a child has lived in this stage of accountability long enough to learn to control himself along the lines for which he is held to account, when he will thus make himself do, at least measurably, what is expected of him, he has entered the next higher stage of responsibility. He begins now to hold himself responsible for doing what, according to his elders, he *ought* to do. If this growing child is fortunate in his home guidance he will, in this last-named stage, build a *conscience* as the correlative of his sense of responsibility. By *conscience* we mean the tendency of a person to hold himself consciously responsible for doing or not doing certain specified things thus accepted as *right* or *wrong*. To act properly with regard to a recognized *right* or *wrong* becomes a *duty*. To each such *duty* belongs a feeling of *oughtness*. Conscience is the active feeling of *ought* in connection with a recognized *duty*.

WHK PE 94

The form his (Dr Arnold's) enjoyment took is recorded in a letter to his wife, as follows:

> It is almost awful to look at the overwhelming beauty around me, and then think of moral evil; it seems as if heaven and hell, instead of being separated by a great gulf from one another, were absolutely on each other's confines, and indeed not far from every one of us. Might the sense of moral evil be as strong in me as my delight in external beauty, for in a deep sense of moral evil, more perhaps than in anything else, abides a saving knowledge of God! It is not so much to admire moral good; that we may do, and yet not be ourselves conformed to it; but if we really do abhor that which is evil, nor the persons in whom evil resides, but the evil which dwelleth in them, and much more manifestly and certainly to our own knowledge, in our own hearts—this is to have the feeling of God and of Christ, and to have our Spirit in sympathy with the Spirit of God. Alas! how easy to see this and say it—how hard to do it and to feel it! Who is sufficient for these things? No one, but he who feels and really laments his own insufficiency. God bless you, my dearest wife, and our beloved children, now and evermore, through Christ Jesus.

It is pathetic to see this naturally kindly gentleman lashing himself into a mood of sadism, in which he can flog little boys without compunction, and all under the impression that he is conforming to the religion of Love. It is pathetic when we consider the deluded individual; but it is tragic when we think of the generations of cruelty that he put into the world by creating an atmosphere of abhorrence of 'moral evil', which, it will be remembered, includes habitual idleness in children. I shudder when I think of the wars, the tortures, the oppressions, of which upright men have been guilty, under the impression that they were righteously castigating 'moral evil'. Mercifully, educators no longer regard little children as limbs of Satan. There is still too much of this view in dealings with adults, particularly in the punishment of crime; but in the nursery and the school it has almost disappeared.

There is an opposite error to Dr Arnold's, far less pernicious, but still scientifically an error, and that is the belief that children are naturally virtuous, and are only corrupted by the spectacle of their elders' vices. This view is traditionally associated with Rousseau; perhaps he held it in the abstract, but when one reads *Emile* one finds that the pupil stood in need of much moral training before he became the paragon that the system was designed to produce. The fact is that children are not naturally either 'good' or 'bad'. They are born with only reflexes and a few instincts; out of these, by the action of the environment, habits are produced, which may be either healthy or morbid. Which they are to be depends chiefly upon the wisdom of mothers or nurses, the child's nature being, at first, almost incredibly malleable. In the immense majority of children there is the raw material of a good citizen, and also the raw material of a criminal. Scientific psychology shows that flogging on week-days and sermons on Sundays do not constitute the ideal technique for the production of virtue. But it is not to be inferred that there is no technique for this purpose. It is difficult to resist Samuel Butler's view that the educators of former times took a pleasure in torturing children; otherwise it is hard to see how they can have persisted so long in inflicting useless misery. It is not difficult to make a healthy child happy, and most children will be healthy if their minds and bodies are properly tended. Happiness in childhood is absolutely necessary to the production of the best type of human being. Habitual idleness, which Dr Arnold regarded as a form of 'moral evil', will not exist if the child is made to feel that its education is teaching it something worth knowing.[1] But if the knowledge imparted is worthless, and those who impart it appear as cruel tyrants, the child will naturally behave like Chekhov's kitten. The spontaneous wish to learn, which every normal child possesses, as shown in its efforts to walk and talk, should be the driving-force in education. The substitution of this driving-force for the rod is one of the great advances of our time.

This brings me to the last point which I wish to notice in this preliminary survey of modern tendencies—I mean the greater attention paid to infancy. This is closely connected with the change in our ideas as to the training of character. The old idea was that virtue depends essentially upon *will*: we were supposed to be full of bad desires, which we controlled by an abstract faculty of volition. It was apparently regarded as impossible to root out bad desires: all we could do was to control them. The situation was exactly analogous to that of the criminal and the police. No one supposed that a society without would-be criminals was possible; the most that could be done was to have such an efficient police force that most people would be afraid to commit crimes, and the few exceptions would be caught and punished. The modern psychological criminologist is not content with this view; he believes that the impulse to crime could, in most cases, be prevented

[1] Probably many of Dr Arnold's pupils suffered from adenoids, for which no medical man would prescribe flogging, although they cause habitual idleness.

from developing by suitable education. And what applies to society applies also to the individual. Children, especially, wish to be liked by their elders and their companions; they have, as a rule, impulses which can be developed in good or bad directions according to the situations in which they find themselves. Moreover, they are at an age at which the formation of new habits is still easy; and good habits can make a great part of virtue almost automatic. On the other hand, the older type of virtue, which left bad desires rampant, and merely used will-power to check their manifestations, has been found to afford a far from satisfactory method of controlling bad conduct. The bad desires, like a river which has been dammed, find some other outlet which has escaped the watchful eye of the will. The man who, in youth, would have liked to murder his father, finds satisfaction later on in flogging his own son, under the impression that he is chastising 'moral evil'. Theories which justify cruelty almost always have their source in some desire diverted by the will from its natural channel, driven underground, and at last emerging unrecognized as hatred of sin or something equally respectable. The control of bad desires by the will, therefore, though necessary on occasion, is inadequate as a technique of virtue.

BR OE 24–6

Freedom

Authority in education is to some extent unavoidable, and those who educate have to find a way of exercising authority in accordance with the *spirit* of liberty.

Where authority is unavoidable, what is needed is *reverence.* A man who is to educate really well, and is to make the young grow and develop into their full stature, must be filled through and through with the spirit of reverence. It is reverence towards others that is lacking in those who advocate machine-made cast-iron systems: militarism, capitalism, Fabian scientific organization, and all the other prisons into which reformers and reactionaries try to force the human spirit. In education, with its codes of rules emanating from a Government office, its large classes and fixed curriculum and overworked teachers, its determination to produce a dead level of glib mediocrity, the lack of reverence for the child is all but universal. Reverence requires imagination and vital warmth; it requires most imagination in respect of those who have least actual achievement or power. The child is weak and superficially foolish, the teacher is strong, and in an every-day sense wiser than the child. The teacher without reverence, or the bureaucrat without reverence, easily despises the child for these outward inferiorities. He thinks it is his duty to 'mould' the child: in imagination he is the potter with the clay. And so he gives to the child some unnatural shape, which hardens with age, producing strains and spiritual dissatisfactions, out of which grow cruelty and envy, and the belief that others must be compelled to undergo the same distortions.

The man who has reverence will not think it is his duty to 'mould' the young. He feels in all that lives, but especially in human beings, and most of all in children, something sacred, indefinable, unlimited, something individual and strangely precious, the growing principle of life, an embodied fragment of the dumb striving of the world. In the presence of a child he feels an unaccountable humility—a humility not easily defensible on any rational ground, and yet somehow nearer to wisdom than the easy self-confidence of many parents and teachers. The outward helplessness of the child and the appeal of dependence make him conscious of the responsibility of a trust. His imagination shows him what the child may become, for good or evil, how its impulses may be developed or thwarted, how its hopes must be dimmed and the life in it grow less living, how its trust will be bruised and its quick desires replaced by brooding will. All this gives him a longing to help the child in its own battle; he would equip and strengthen it, not for some outside end proposed by the State or by any other impersonal authority, but for the ends which the child's own spirit is obscurely seeking. The man who feels this can wield the authority of an educator without infringing the principle of liberty.

It is not in a spirit of reverence that education is conducted by States and Churches and the great institutions that are subservient to them. What is considered in education is hardly ever the boy or girl, the young man or young woman, but almost always, in some form, the maintenance of the existing order. When the individual is considered, it is almost exclusively with a view to worldly success—making money or achieving a good position. To be ordinary and to acquire the art of getting on, is the ideal which is set before the youthful mind, except by a few rare teachers who have enough energy of belief to break through the system within which they are expected to work. Almost all education has a political motive: it aims at strengthening some group, national or religious or even social, in the competition with other groups. It is this motive, in the main, which determines the subjects taught, the knowledge offered and the knowledge withheld, and also decides what mental habits the pupils are expected to acquire. Hardly anything is done to foster the inward growth of mind and spirit; in fact, those who have had most education are very often atrophied in their mental and spiritual life, devoid of impulse, and possessing only certain mechanical aptitudes which take the place of living thought.

BR PSR 102–4

The point is, *freedom cannot be given.* It is taken by the child. Freedom involves discovery and invention, neither of which by their very nature can be embodied in any system. Freedom demands the privilege of conscious wrongdoing, and above all things freedom cannot exist in the presence of authoritative punishments.

It remains true, however, that up to the age of eighteen, boys and girls do need some amount of dependence, a substitute for father and mother to whom they can go for advice. The quality of this relationship, and the limits of it, will depend, of course, upon the relations which have been gradually built up in the unconscious mind to the real father and the real mother. For to the illogical unconscious mind of the pupil, the teacher, standing *in loco parentis, is* father or *is* mother; the tag quoted covers a field of unconscious relationship for every pupil to every master and every mistress wider than the lawyers dreamed who made the phrase. Each child will project on to each master or mistress its own habitual attitude to father or to mother. The teacher of a class thus has to behave like twenty-five or forty different parents (for he has a different relationship to every child), and this is not possible, except in private intercourse. For though the teacher may establish relations of sympathy with the individual, he cannot get this relationship at any one time with everyone at once. Therefore the only way to carry on a class is to work through the crowd mind. But, though the teacher *can* in this way become a group leader, yet, if his attitude to the group is one of command, he will only increase its dislike both of himself and of his subject. A group of children is a crowd with a common emotion (the only communion inside a group is unconscious communion, through feeling, not reason), and this emotion, based on their previous experience, is nearly always of dislike for the teacher, having been carried forward from their experience of parental authority as something limiting their freedom. For in all children there will be some, and in many children much, resistance to authority; therefore all attempts to impose knowledge by authority call up contra-suggestion to defeat them. The very institutionalism of the school makes the child dislike learning; that is why it is so important for him that for the information which is given him he should have a definite want, a social or group interest in getting it which shall be something quite different from both his own and his group's reactions to authority. Until, therefore, the teacher can become a *member* of the crowd, and do away with the emotional attitude of the crowd by himself resigning his own authoritarian position, he will find both disciplinary problems and a dislike of his own instructions. It is his unconscious emotional attitude which will determine the group's reaction to him. The mere hearty affection to unfrock himself is useless; but if by unconscious sympathy he drops from status, and incorporates himself in the group, then the group attitude to his arithmetic will be favourable; for when he has done this the individual can regain conscious control of his intelligence and 'learn' decimals with an emotional sympathy warmed by the cooperation of the group. . . .

HL TPT 112–3

Our aim was to impose nothing on the child, but in actual practice freedom was limited. No general vote was invited to decide who should cook and what should be cooked. New staff were appointed without any reference to or consultation with children or for that matter other staff. The rough and ready aim was to have freedom to live one's own life so long as one did not disturb the freedom of others . . . and it was incumbent on us to distinguish freedom from licence, a task that many adults cannot tackle. At a venture I can say that, on the average, children who came to school early, up to—say—seven, knew the difference between freedom and licence, while older incomers took a long time to realize where the borderline lay. Sometimes new staff had a licence attitude also. In the school's beginning it was a matter of excitement to get a new pupil: how will she react? Will he go unwashed for weeks? The excitement has long worn off, for today we have a pretty good notion of how any new pupil will react to sudden freedom. He will, say at the age of thirteen, swear a lot, smoke a lot, be cheeky and at the same time afraid of being punished for his impudence; he may go unwashed for days and certainly will lie abed mornings, even although he thus misses his breakfast which is cleared away at nine. He will seldom show any desire to create, but often a strong one to be destructive. He will lock the bathroom door, that is if he thinks of having a bath, and he will snigger guiltily if he sees a boy or girl run along a passage naked. If he has had a strict father he will look at me with some fear, will soon realize that I am not the stern father type, and possibly begin to hit me playfully. Thirty years of that reaction from moulded, repressed boys and girls have made me uneasy at taking problem children of that age. Self-sacrifice is especially unwelcome when one is pulling patriarchally spoiled chestnuts out of the fire.

One surprising feature in Public School character formation was its lack of depth in such things as manners. Boys came with beautiful manners and soon dropped them completely, realizing no doubt that their insincerity was out of place in Summerhill. Indeed for every child from whatever type of school the gradual dropping of insincerity in voice, manner, action became the norm. Pupils from State schools generally took longest to drop their insincerity and cheek. Free children are never cheeky, nor indeed are semi-free ones. Freedom works slowly; it may take several years for a child to understand what it means, and anyone who expects quick results is an incurable optimist. And freedom works best with clever children. I should like to be able to say that, since freedom touches the emotions primarily, all children, intelligent and dull, react equally to it. I cannot say it. One sees the difference in the matter of lessons. Every child under freedom plays most of the time for years, but the bright one, when the time comes, will sit down and tackle the School Certificate Exam, and in a little over two years cover the work that disciplined children take years to cover. The orthodox academic teacher holds that exams will be passed only if discipline keeps the candidate's nose to the grindstone. Our results prove that that is a fallacy with bright pupils; under freedom it is only the bright ones who can concentrate on intensive study, a most difficult thing to do in a community in which so many counter-attractive activities are going on. I know that comparatively poor material passes exams under discipline, but I wonder what becomes of the passers later on. If all schools were free and all lessons were optional, I fancy that children would find their own level, and indifferent scholars who, under discipline, scrape through college or university and become unimaginative teachers and doctors and lawyers, would possibly be good mechanics or bricklayers or policemen. We have found that the boy who cannot or will not learn to read until he is—say—fifteen, is always a mechanical boy who later on becomes a good engineer or electrician, but we should not dare dogmatize about girls who never go to lessons . . . especially mathematics and physics. Often they spend much time with needlework and some take up dressmaking and designing later. Anyway it is an absurd curriculum that makes a prospective dress-cutter study quadratic equations or Boyle's Law.

Coming to a part of freedom much more important than lessons, did we find that clever children were better citizens than their duller brothers and sisters? Were they more communally minded, or to put it concretely did the clever ones voluntarily pick up the litter that their less gifted companions ignored? I am sorry to say that they did not. One of the hard-to-accept features of free children is that they do not like gardening or indeed any manual labour that has no play aim. If a general vote gets them to go out and dig potatoes, they go unwillingly because the end result is too far away and has no play component, but the same crowd will spend weeks laboriously digging deep holes and trenches because they want to play some elaborate underground game. For years these holes and tunnels have been nightmares to me even though the older pupils were always helpful in making them safe for the younger dare-devils.

Here a parenthesis about the limits of freedom when safety is concerned. It is no joke to be in charge of other people's children, yet there is an important asset in the commonsense of children. When our school meeting passes a law that no one must bathe in the sea without a life-saver, there is not a child in the school who will break the law. It is the border-line case that bothers, the climbing of trees for instance. To ban tree-climbing would be wrong and futile, for it is the right of every child to climb trees. A boy of seven recently fell about twenty-four feet on his head and fractured his skull. Luckily he survived. Only a fool in charge of young children would allow unbarred high bedroom windows, or an unprotected nursery fire. Yet too often young enthusiasts for freedom come to my school as visitors, and exclaim at our lack of freedom in locking a lab poison cupboard or prohibiting fooling about with the fire escape. The whole freedom movement is marred and despised because so many freedom fans have not their feet on the ground. One such protested to me recently because I shouted sternly at a problem boy of seven who was kicking my office door. His idea was that I should smile and tolerate the noise until the child should live out his desire to bang doors. It is true that I spent a good few years of my life patiently tolerating the destructive behaviour of problem haters, but as their psychological doctor not their fellow citizen. If my head had been in the clouds I should never have been able to see them to help them.

To return to the children's reaction to emotional freedom, all, clever and not so clever, gained something that they had not had before, a something that is almost indefinable. Its chief outer sign was a great increase in sincerity and charity, added to a lessening of aggression. I think the Freudians have made a great mistake about aggression; they look for it in every child, every adult, and of course they find it, for it is there all right, put there by character-moulding and suppression. The Freudians studied the wrong children. When children are not under fear and discipline they are not patently aggressive; only once in thirty years of Summerhill have I seen a fight with bloody noses. The aggressive child, the small bully we always have, and no amount of freedom at school can completely counteract the influence of a bad home. Character acquired in the first months or years of life can be modified by freedom, but it can never be completely changed.

ASN FC 33–6

Freedom, why and how much

'Growing is the test. If they learn how to make better moral distinctions and if they better act accordingly, they are growing, and then they are using their freedom wisely. If not, they are not so using it.'

'But may not one learn from his mistakes?'

'Most certainly, and I mean to include that. What I demand is that the child shall grow in the matter at hand.'

Why child purposing

'Then, if we may go back, in this matter of child purposing, you first and mainly wish whole-hearted purposing of what a child is doing because the learning results are then likely to be best?'

'Yes, up to today that has been our main contention. That is what we have mainly meant when we have hitherto advocated whole-hearted child purposing.'

'And this is quite consistent with teacher suggestion, provided the child does whole-heartedly accept the teacher's suggestion?'

'Quite so.'

'But now you wish to take a step further and say that a child should, under wise teacher guidance and control, practice choosing?'

'Yes, granted wise guidance, to practice choosing is the best promise for growth in power to choose.'

'And in this you would give all the freedom the children can use successfully?'

'Yes, that's it.'

'And by "successfully" you mean that they are to grow in making wise and ethical choices?'

'Yes, growth is always the test. If that is taking place properly, we are on the right line. If not, something is wrong.'

WHK FM 210

These people in their hearts reject freedom of speech and freedom of study because they themselves already have 'the truth' and these freedoms might if followed 'subvert' their 'truth.' It is from this point of view that they are so anxious to have 'loyalty oaths' exacted of teachers. Without exactly knowing it they tend to look on political constitutions as essentially fixed and unchanging. Such people have great difficulty in conceiving of dynamic loyalty, that is, loyalty to the search for what to think; they think only of static loyalty, loyalty to what has already been said. In this way, as one of them declared, 'academic freedom of speech has no place in school, where the youth of our country are taught and their unformed minds are developed.' In other words, teachers must first form the mind of the young through an indoctrination of 'the truth' which 'we' know. Only after the mind has been thus formed so that it cannot later be upset can 'academic freedom' be permissible, because then it is harmless.

What these people do not see is that academic freedom is the democratic educative process itself, where young and old discuss and consider unsettled matters in order thereby to learn through study and concluding how better to study and conclude. Being Tories, and therefore not believing essentially in democracy, they refuse to see that this continued process of study and concluding is of the very essence of democracy.

WHK TS 36

Self-government and democracy

An account of the Little Commonwealth at Evershot, Dorset. Extract from a lecture given by Lane in 1918.

The Little Commonwealth is a co-educational community inhabited by children ranging in age from a few months to nineteen years, those more than thirteen years of age having been committed for a term of years for crime, as to a reformatory—in fact, the Little Commonwealth has recently been certified as a reformatory. The younger children are those who would in any case be subject to institutional care in asylums or orphanages. At the present moment the population of the Commonwealth is five adults, four of whom are women, forty-two boys and girls of fourteen to nineteen years of age, and nine younger children. This population is distributed among three 'families,' grouped by congeniality; each person is free to choose his own place of residence. Boys and girls live in the same families, sharing equally the responsibility for family maintenance and government, as well as the responsibility for the welfare of the younger children. The chief point of difference between the Commonwealth and other reformatories and schools is that in the Commonwealth there are no rules and regulations except those made by the boys and girls themselves. All those who are fourteen years of age and over are citizens, having joint responsibility for the regulation of their lives by the laws and judicial machinery organized and developed by themselves. The adult element studiously avoid any assumption of authority in the community, except in connection with their respective departmental duties as teachers or as supervisors of labour within the economic scheme. The citizens are paid wages in Commonwealth currency for their work in the various departments, and provide their own food, clothing, and recreations to whatever degree of comfort and elegance their earning capacity will permit. The wage paid corresponds to that of the outside world in similar employments. The citizens are occupied chiefly with earning a living, to a regrettable exclusion of any considerable time for formal school-work. This, of course, does not apply to the children under fourteen, who have no work to do other than that chosen by themselves after the school-work is finished.

The improvident citizen, the slacker, if he is unable to pay his own expenses, must be supported from the public treasury, the funds of which are raised by taxation. If a discontented citizen causes any damage, fails to pay for his board, or runs away, the expense of misdemeanour is borne by the taxpayers. If the citizens' court imposes any penalty upon an erring citizen which interferes with his employment, the community must provide him with necessities.

Thus it may be seen that in the Commonwealth there is a direct relationship between prosperity and morality. What better field could there be for the cultivation and growth of a code that is based upon the spontaneous virtues of adolescent human nature? And those virtues have certainly been in evidence during the whole of our four years of existence. The moral standards of the citizen group, as measured by its attitude toward the individual delinquent, have always been wholesome and clear and definite. This is as true of those offences that do not cause any expense to the taxpayer as of those that do. Hence our belief that in spite of the very prominent place in the organization of the Commonwealth occupied by the scheme of economics, the morality of the community is not exclusively of the £ s. d. type. That is, while honesty is the best policy in the Commonwealth as elsewhere, honesty is not entirely a matter of policy. During the first year, while the original group of citizens were assuming their new responsibilities, there were frequent sudden changes in the attitude of the group toward the individual wrongdoer. At times severe penalties were imposed upon him, and then quite suddenly the type of penalties would undergo a marked change. Such punishments as close bounds, fines and other forms of deprivation would almost disappear, the wrongdoer being merely expected to make restitution so far as was possible to the community or individual for any injuries he might have done to property. Each change had causes which are obscure and difficult of diagnosis, but of the highest possible importance in a study of the moral growth of the children.

Perhaps the most interesting period in the short history of the Commonwealth is that of the first few months after a group of about fifteen so-called criminal boys and girls had been collected and the experiment in self-government begun. These boys and girls had no idea of social order. Their conception of material values was most vague. Born and reared in city slums, surrounded on every side by the authority of parents, police and school officials, the victims of an especially narrow and restricted environment, their faculty of self-restraint was almost wholly undeveloped except when in close proximity to some restraining authority. Their idea of social relationships was limited to the primitive form of co-operation for self-protection—against authority. Separately they were passive, subdued and apathetic. Combined or as a group they were aggressive, fearless and anti-social.

It was necessary to employ extraordinary methods to free them from their misconceptions of society and social order. They had a very keen legal sense of right and wrong, but it could not be called a moral code. We said to them, 'You may do as you please,' but they did not believe it. In the presence of us adults they had no initiative, were self-repressed and passive. By themselves they were spontaneous, original, active and resourceful, but usually in a destructive direction. The acknowledged leader was the boy who had the best command of unconventional language, who was most daring in destructive activities, and who assumed the most defiant attitude towards adults. On the whole they were unusually obedient to a direct command or request; but it was the obedience of weakness, not of strength. Their ideals were anti-social. Now the conventional method of altering children's ideals is to suppress their undesirable activities, and by means of some form of primitive treatment to impress our ideals upon them. But the logical method is to dissipate the child's ideal by encouragement of his activities, until he himself discovers its advantages. The latter method was employed in the Commonwealth. I joined the group in its disturbing activities, became one of the gang, and by so doing speedily spoiled the fun. As the recognized authority in the community, my sanction and encouragement of midnight pillow-fights, larder raids and hooliganism did away with the element of danger involved, and it ceased to be fun. Now we were ready to organize in another direction, and did so. The citizens began to take interest in the more serious occupations at hand. The ideal of the group had altered. They helped with the work, and began to caution the more obstreperous about their conduct. Gradually they arrived at the point where the need for formal rules and laws was felt. They instituted not only a form of parliamentary procedure, under which rules were enacted, but also a judicial procedure by which violations of rules were dealt with. It is in the citizens' court that one may get into closer touch with the spirit of the Commonwealth than in any other community function, and it is here that I look for the true spiritual expressions of our boys and girls. Now I will readily admit that in the greater community one does not, as a rule, search in the courts for manifestations of the spiritual life of a people, but that is because courts are legal institutions rather than the mouthpiece of a public code of morality as in the Commonwealth. All the citizens of the Commonwealth attend courts, and the highest judicial authority is the referendum. Disputed points as between the citizen judge and an offender are decided by public opinion by means of the roll-call. Each citizen must express an opinion.

HL TPT 188–93

When we founded the school we resolved to have no government from above, and self-government was, as it were, forced on the children. Much has been said and written about the iniquity of 'forcing' self-government on children. Some time ago at a meeting of progressive school teachers in London the theme was self-government. Two teachers from progressive schools got up and each told the same tale—that they had given their children self-government, and in three weeks the children came and beseeched them to bring back the old way of benevolent adult authority. Currie of Dartington Hall sat by me.

'For God's sake, Neill,' he said impatiently, 'get up and tell them what self-government is. You are the only man in the room who has had it for years.'

I declined.

'What's the good?' I said wearily. 'They don't want to believe that self-government can succeed.'

The school that has no self-government should not be called a progressive school at all. It is a compromise school. You cannot have progression unless children feel completely free to govern their own social life. When there is a boss, freedom is not there, and this applies more to the benevolent boss than to the disciplinarian. The child of spirit can rebel against the hard boss, but the soft boss merely makes him impotently soft himself.

Is it worthwhile giving the arguments for self-government? I wonder if it is. All that is necessary to say is that one weekly general meeting is, in my opinion, of more value than a week's curriculum of school subjects. The educational value of practical civics cannot be over-emphasized. The child realizes the value of self-government and in Summerhill the pupils would fight to the death for their right to govern themselves.

Our system of self-government has gone through various phases and changes. When we had six pupils it was a kind of family affair. If Derrick punched Inge she would call a meeting and we would all sit round and give our opinions. We had no jury system; the verdict and sentence were given by show of hands. As the school grew bigger this family method gradually changed, and the first change was the election of a chairman. Following that came trial by jury, a jury elected on the spot by the chairman. The culprit had the right of challenging any member of the jury, but this seldom happened: only occasionally would one hear the protest: 'I won't have Bill on the jury, for he's a pal of Pat's (Pat being the plaintiff who got punched).'

During the last year or two we have had another form of government. At the beginning of each term a government of five is elected by vote. This sort of cabinet deals with all cases of charges and acts as a jury, giving punishment. The cases are read out at the general Saturday night meeting, and the verdicts are announced. Here is a typical example of such a procedure:

Jim has taken the pedals from Jack's cycle because his own cycle is a dud and he wants to go away with some others for a week-end hike. The government after due consideration of the evidence announces that Jim has to replace the pedals and be forbidden to go on the hike. The chairman says: 'Any objections?'

Jim gets up and shouts that there jolly well are (only his adjective isn't exactly 'jolly').

'This isn't fair,' he cries. 'I didn't know that Jack ever used his old crock of a grid; it has been kicking about among the bushes for days. I don't mind shoving his pedals back but I think the punishment unfair. I don't want to have the hike cut out.'

Follows a breezy discussion. In this it transpires that Jim should have a weekly allowance from home, but it hasn't come for six weeks and he hasn't a bean. The meeting votes that the sentence be quashed and it is duly quashed. But what to do about Jim?

Finally it is decided to open a subscription fund to put Jim's bike in order . . . and he sets off on his hike happily.

Usually the government's verdict is accepted both by the culprit and the community. On appeal I cannot remember a government sentence being increased. The ordinary procedure on an appeal is for the chairman (nearly always a pupil) to elect a jury to decide the appeal, and in the case of Jim and the bike the jury had disagreed and had left the decision to the general vote.

Certain classes of offences come under the automatic fine rule. If you ride another's cycle without permission there is an automatic fine of sixpence. Swearing down town (but you can swear as much as you like in the school grounds), bad behaviour in the cinema, climbing on roofs, throwing food in the dining-room, these and others are automatic fine rules. Punishments are nearly always fines . . . half a pocket-money or miss a cinema. When, recently, Paxton Chadwick (Chad) was tried for riding Ginger's bike without permission, he and two other members of the staff, who had also ridden it, were ordered to push each other on Ginger's bike ten times round the front lawn. Four small boys who climbed the ladder of the builders erecting the new workshop were ordered to climb up and down the ladder for ten minutes on end. A jury never seeks advice from an adult, well, I can remember only one occasion when it was done. Three girls had raided the kitchen larder. The government fined them their pocket-money. They raided the larder again that night, and the jury fined them a cinema. They raided it once more, and the government was gravelled what to do. The foreman consulted me.

'Give them tuppence reward each,' I suggested.

'What? Why, man, you'll have the whole school raiding the larder if we do that.'

'You won't,' I said. 'Try it.'

They tried it. Two of the girls refused to take the money, and all three were heard to declare that they would never raid the larder again . . . they didn't for about two months all the same.

If I am giving the impression that our self-government is only a police court I am giving a wrong impression. It sometimes happens that no one has broken a law during the week. The function of the government is to make all laws and to discuss social features of the community. At the beginning of each term bedtime rules are made by vote . . . you go to bed according to your age. Then questions of general behaviour come up. Sports committees have to be elected, end of term dance committee, the theatre committee, bedtime officers, down-town officers (who report any disgraceful behaviour out of the school boundary). The most exciting subject ever brought up is that of food. I have more than once wakened up a dull meeting by proposing that second helpings be abolished. Any sign of kitchen favouritism in the matter of food is severely handled, but when the kitchen brings up the question of food wastage the meeting is not much interested. Children's attitude to food is essentially a personal and self-centred one.

ASN TOS 31–4

Is your self-government phoney? David Holbrook would seem to think it's no good.

David Holbrook in an article in *Id*, the journal of the Summerhill Society writes: 'I think of the children sitting on the floor of Neill's school voting on their own rules: in a way this is asking children to do what the adults should do for them.' David was sixteen when he last saw a school meeting.

I do not know where to begin with this criticism, for it reaches down to fundamentals. It questions self-regulation in general. It really asks: how far can a child decide social matters for itself? We all know the other way, the usual way.... Your elders know better, so do as you are told. Some of us ask if elders do know better. In Summerhill I know better about some things. I don't ask the pupils to appoint a teacher; Ena does not ask what food they shall have. I decide about fire escapes, Ena about health rules. We buy and repair the furniture; we decide what textbooks should be bought. None of these factors come into self-government. Nor do the pupils want them to. Self-government to them means dealing with situations that arise in their communal life; they can say what they like, vote how they like in a meeting, and they never wait to see how the staff votes. True a member of the staff can often get his or her motion carried, but the motion is judged on its merits. I have proposed scores of motions in my time and had them outvoted. We never ask children to decide on things that are beyond their ability to grasp.

Good self-government arises when we have a goodly sprinkling of older pupils, but they should be pupils who have grown up in the system. When we enrol boys and girls of fifteen and over they do not help the self-government; they have too many repressions to let off, they do not grasp freedom unconsciously as adolescents do who have had seven or eight years in the school. So that sometimes today our government has too much of the staff element in it. If someone throws food all over the dining-room walls an older pupil will raise the matter in a meeting, that is if he or she is an old stager, but recently when we had an influx of teenagers who had no social feeling about food throwing, one of the staff would bring the matter up. We all feel that this is bad, but under the circumstances inevitable.

Self-government is maybe phoney when there are only young children. Since we began with five children we learned the hard way that very young children have not the ability to make rules impartially, yet the strange feature is that all the very young kindergarten ones comes to every meeting and register their votes, and often make good speeches before they can read and write.

What part should adults play in self-government? They should not lead; they should have the gift of standing more or less outside. When a child is charged with some breach of the rules I make it a point never to vote for or against—say—a sixpenny fine. I sometimes have to have a private talk with a pupil (a P.L.) and it would be impossible for me to vote that Willie be fined for riding Tom's bike, and then be his therapist next day.

I think the test of the value of self-government lies in the determination of the pupils to retain it. Any suggestion of abolishing it, even of limiting its powers is met by a very strong reaction. I have suggested abolition twice but would not dare ever to do so again.

I grant that democracy is far from perfect. Majority rule is not too satisfactory, but I can see no alternative barring dictatorship. The minority always suffers. What has surprised me for years has been that our school minority accepts the majority verdict; if there is a refusal to accept it it comes from some lad of fifteen who has just come and cannot see why he has to obey 'what a crowd of bloody kids vote on'.

Is the whole set-up phoney in that children make laws and don't keep them? Some laws are often broken, especially the bedtime law, yet I am sure that if I made the laws more of them would be broken, for then the natural rebellion against father would come in. In a fear boarding school there is law-breaking in the dormitories at nights. 'The Law makes the crime.'

On the whole the laws in Summerhill are pretty well kept, partly, maybe mainly, because children are so charitable with each other. I have marvelled for forty-five years about the sense of justice they show. A boy is charged for bullying and reprimanded by the meeting. At the next meeting he brings up a trumpery charge against the bullyee. The meeting spots that it is a revenge charge and tells him so.

Someone wrote that our self-government is a fake because the staff really makes the rules and pretends that the pupils make them by a show of hands. That is just a libel as any pupil, past or present, would know. As I have said many a time they will vote for a law on its own merits whoever proposes it. I have more than once proposed that the loud gram be played only in the evenings. I am always outvoted. One of the staff will bring up the wastage of good food . . . we have a tuckshop just outside the grounds, and often a child will stoke up on ice lollies and come to lunch and leave it. The staff proposal may be that anyone leaving his or her lunch should be deprived of lunch next day. The motion is never carried. Again and again I have proposed that money sent to pupils during term should be pooled and divided equally. This is always negatived; all the ones with the least pocket money from home vote against it. But I have said enough to show that our democracy is not fake I hope.

ASN TS 32–5

We discussed earlier how freedom to purpose is the test of actual respect for personality. We wish here to see (i) how purposeful activity successfully pursued tends to build self-respect in the person who is engaged in such activity; further, how a regime of group purposing, properly directed, gives unequalled opportunity to (ii) build respect for the personality of others; and (iii) to develop ability to discover possibilities through shared search and at the same time develop cooperative attitudes and methods of discussing, conferring, making shared decisions on such a give-and-take basis as makes for a proper respect for others. These three points we now consider in order.

1. *Freedom to purpose is essential to building of self-respect. Properly directed it builds not only self-respect, but also ability to*

choose wisely and to accept responsibility. To purpose wisely and to pursue purposes appropriately means to choose one's ends and means intelligently and ethically. For pupils thus to accept, under wise teacher guidance, responsibility for their activity and its outcomes will tend, in the degree the work is well done and properly appreciated, to build the following concomitant learnings: greater carefulness in choosing both ends and means; increased thoughtfulness and persistence in pursuing endeavors; better practical judgment in such matters; growth of confidence in ability to succeed and so win justified approval of others. To build these various attitudes is—to that extent—to build a proper respect for oneself as capable within the areas thus conquered and at the same time an increasing acceptance of responsibility for one's acts.

2. *A regime of group purposes wisely and successfully directed gives opportunity for building respect for the personality of others.* In fact it seems probable that nothing can equal such a regime for producing this result. Given a class of pupils mature enough to purpose together and adequate opportunity to form and pursue purposes which to them seem challenging and significant, we can be reasonably sure that each who enters heartily into the effort will build respect for all the others who join in the effort with like heartiness and deport themselves with reasonable consideration of the rest. And, further, to give youth the chance thus to work together at what they think is worth-while is the best known way of building interest in their work and of evoking their varied powers of thought and action.

Probably the one single factor that most militates against success at such purposeful activity in school is the set demand of the school authorities for acquiring fixed-in-advance subject matter according to a prearranged time table. In the degree that the school is run on this basis is a regime of purposeful activity practically impossible of attainment.

Granted flexibility enough in school requirements, and reasonably sympathetic and wise management on the part of teachers, it is possible to get any typical group of children or youth very happily at work along these lines: (i) choosing ever better projects and activities and experiences to undertake; (ii) planning how to manage and apportioning the work among all the participants; (iii) executing the plans, changing these if developments so direct; and (iv) judging the results, not with intent to apportion praise or blame or even just credit, but to learn how to carry on such an experience better next time and to get from this one experience any suggestions of further things to do.

Care should be taken that individuals are in no sense pitted against each other to win credit or praise, that instead attention and interest are directed to getting the work itself well done, with due appreciation, to be sure, of good work everywhere. In the degree that these conditions are met it is probable that interest in such work will increase, together with interest in successful work of ever finer quality; that mutual appreciation will be built by each one for the others working with him, as persons who can be counted on to do the right thing at the right time. It should be recognized that these results will not necessarily come of themselves, that the teacher will have to work for them. It is also true that there may be some small number who will not successfully fit in with the rest; but the probability is that under wise and sympathetic guidance few will be able to resist the constructive tendencies here outlined....

3 *Such a regime of group purposing will, under wise guidance, build in the individuals of the group definite ability to work together in a democratic framework of shared study and decision.* They will learn how to get information in many varied ways and devise creative means to their ends; they will build increasing acceptance of responsibility to take others into account; they will also develop real skill in discussing to find out what to think and do. In fact they will develop all these traits to a degree incredible to teachers used only to children made antagonistic and cranky by formal school treatment.

This plan of constructive conferring at purposeful enterprises is our chance to make democracy work. The future will make demands on democracy far harder to meet than in the past. We must make the One World work together; and democracy is the only basis on which this is possible. As discussed earlier we are troubled at present because one side of our split world does not know how to discuss inquiringly and to take due account of the values that others feel. But if we take stock of ourselves we find that few of us know how to discuss questions without getting angry. Still fewer know how to discuss them in a way to get at the real merits of what is at issue, to pool ideas and resources, and to give sincere consideration to the ideas and values of others; and fewer still demand this of themselves and others as the only honest thing to do.

If we are to make democracy work, our schools must remake themselves; and this consciously shared effort at decision and executing is an essential part of the remaking. If we can begin this kind of thing in the lower elementary school and continue it from there to the upper elementary, the high school, and the college, we can greatly improve the social process in our country and ultimately in the world. If labor and management had only learned how to confer honestly on a basis of getting at the best possible solution of their difficulties, we would have been spared many if not most of our industrial quarrels. If our schools worked at this sort of thing sufficiently to build it into the minds and characters of nine tenths of our people, instead of as now probably in no more than one twentieth, we could remake our civilization. With more discerning citizens many of the worst of our newspapers would have to go out of business, and the best could raise their standards still higher. Our political campaigns could and would be conducted on a higher level. Congress would argue more honestly and legislate far more effectively.

It can be done, but not in schools run as they are now commonly run. Practice in the intelligent pursuit of group purposes is our key to the future.

WHK PE 259–62

'Do I correctly understand that we are to think of education as all the influences that mold one's life and that just plain natural living in those older and simpler days came fairly close to giving the whole of the all-round training then needed for such a simple life?'

'Yes, that's well said.'

'And that now with so many lines of work having left the home for the factory—large and distant factories at that—the home and community no longer supply the same sort of education they once did?'

'Yes. Or you might say it in this way—that the school in that day had but a small part of the total educational work to carry. Now it has a much larger part.'

'I don't see why you put all these things on the school.'

The school must accept duties other agencies relinquish

'For the simple reason that they are not otherwise cared for.

The school is the social institution made to care for all that would otherwise be neglected. You may not like it, but it is a fact. The school is the residuary legatee so far as concerns social duties. What the others won't care for, the school must undertake.'

'Don't you think it weakens the family to have the school take up so many things that the family should care for?'

'Don't misunderstand me. I am trying neither to impoverish the home nor to relieve it of its proper duties. What I am trying to do is to recognize facts. The present family faces a different situation from the old family. I would strengthen the family in any way feasible, but we must not refuse to do the best possible by all the children. What the family cannot or will not do, the school must do. Possibly the rising generation, if better educated to face present conditions, will raise the status of family life in the next generation.'

'And are the other educative institutions—the church, the community, business life—in similar fashion yielding their former educative functions to the school?'

Business as an educative agency

'No single answer will suffice. Much of business demands better general education than formerly, but business itself offers less in the way of apprenticeship. "No admission" signs indicate too that childish observers are not welcome. Putting it all together, it seems fair to say that business on the whole follows the general trend; it demends relatively more and offers relatively less. The schools must make good the difference.'

'How about the community?'

'I think we have already answered that. Social life is vastly more complex, which means at one and the same time that it too demands more and offers relatively less.'

WHK FM 260–1

Democracy, both as a term and as a conception, shows through the ages many historic changes of meaning and scope. Originally the term meant a kind of government, government by the citizens generally as opposed to government by a king or an oligarchy. Henceforth the individual citizen would enjoy freedom from an arbitrary control by a king, and instead would himself share in determining the management of law and order. At the founding of our own nation it was the freedom aspect that was perhaps most active—freedom from the rule of Great Britain.

In our day the meaning of democracy, while thus taking its start in government, is increasingly widened beyond government to indicate a way of life, a quality of associated living based on active respect for human personality, and this along all the lines that consistently go to make up desirable living. In this sense democracy becomes, practically, the effort to run society on the basis of ethics and respect for human personality. And this growth in the meaning and application of democracy is still actively in process in the world today.

The development of the meaning of democracy beyond the area of actual government has, it appears, grown out of a more extended consideration of the proper aim of democratic government, namely, to ensure to each individual the fair and equal chance to live fully as a conscious and self-directing person. Such an emphasis naturally carries the aim of democracy beyond those areas of life in which the compulsions of government are suitable into certain wider areas where compulsion is too crude to be effective, where instead the inner attitude of moral obligation must be our reliance. It is with this stress on inner attitude that democracy reaches beyond mere government and becomes instead a way of life.

The term *democracy* is thus used in two senses. On the one hand, it indicates a kind of government, a government of the people. On the other hand, it means a way of life, a kind and quality of associated living in which sensitive moral principles assert the right to control individual and group conduct. It is worthy of note, however, that in either sense democracy involves control, the control of both individual and group conduct for the good of all affected. In the first sense, the control is by the coercion of government; in the second sense, the control is internal, the demand of intelligence and conscience upon the individual himself to obey and serve the varied calls of a social morality. It may be added that neither control is to repress any proper individuality, but always to allow expression of individuality as effectively as possible in all relationships.

WHK PE 126–7

The results of these two views in practice are very different. According to the former view, when the majority has decided in favour of some opinion, no other must be allowed to be expressed, or if expressed at all must be confined to obscure and uninfluential channels. According to the other view, minority opinions should be given the same opportunities for expression as are given to majority opinions, but only in a lesser degree.

This applies in particular to teaching. A man or woman who is to hold a teaching post under the State should not be required to express majority opinions, though naturally a majority of teachers will do so. Uniformity in the opinions expressed by teachers is not only not to be sought, but is, if possible, to be avoided, since diversity of opinion among preceptors is essential to any sound education. No man can pass as educated who has heard only one side on questions as to which the public is divided. One of the most important things to teach in the educational establishments of a democracy is the power of weighing arguments, and the open mind which is prepared in advance to accept whichever side appears the more reasonable. As soon as a censorship is imposed upon the opinions which teachers may avow, education ceases to serve this purpose and tends to produce, instead of a nation of men, a herd of fanatical bigots. . . .

There are two questions which are not sufficiently distinguished: the one as to the best form of government; the other as to the functions of government. I have no doubt in my mind that democracy is the best *form* of government, but it may go as much astray as any other form in regard to the *functions* of government. There are certain matters on which common action is necessary; as to these, the common action should be decided by the majority. There are other matters on which a common decision is neither necessary nor desirable. These matters include the sphere of opinion.

BR WIC 137–8

Competition

Of the dominant ideals of the nineteenth century, some have survived into our age, and some have not. Those that have survived have, for the most part, a more restricted field of application in our day than they had a hundred years ago. And of these the ideal of competition is a good example. It is, I think, a mistake to regard the belief in competition as due to Darwinism. The opposite is really the case: it was Darwinism that was due to belief in competition. The modern biologist, while he still believes in evolution, has much less belief in competition as its motive force than Darwin had; and this change reflects the change which has come over the economic structure of society. Industrialism began with large numbers of small firms all competing against each other, and at first with very little help from the State, which was still agricultural and aristocratic. Early industrialists, therefore, believed in self-help, *laissez faire*, and competition. From industry, the idea of competition spread to other spheres. Darwin persuaded men that competition between different forms of life was the cause of evolutionary progress. Educationists became persuaded that competition in the class-room was the best way to promote industry among the scholars. Belief in free competition was used by employers as an argument against trade-unionism, and is still so used in the backward parts of America. But competition between capitalists gradually diminished. The tendency has been for the whole of one industry to combine nationally, so that competition has become mainly between nations, and much less than formerly between different firms within a given nation. Meantime, it has naturally been the endeavour of capitalists, while combining themselves, to hinder combinations as much as they could where their employees were concerned. Their motto has been: 'United we stand; divided they fall.' Free competition has thus been preserved as a Great Ideal in all provinces of human life, except in the activities of industrial magnates. Where the industrial magnates are concerned, the competition is national, and therefore takes the form of encouraging patriotism.

In education, the ideal of competition has had two kinds of bad effects. On the one hand, it has led to the teaching of respect for competition as opposed to co-operation, especially in international affairs; and on the other hand, it has led to a vast system of competitiveness in the class-room, and in the endeavour to secure scholarships, and subsequently in the search for jobs. This last stage has been somewhat softened, where wage-earners are concerned, by trade-unionism. But among professional men it has retained all its unmitigated severity.

One of the worst defects of the belief in competition in education is that it has led, especially with the best pupils, to a great deal of over-education.

BR ESO 160-3

The games of later years differ from those of early childhood by the fact that they become increasingly competitive. At first, a child's play is solitary; it is difficult for an infant to join in the games of older brothers and sisters. But collective play, as soon as it becomes possible, is so much more delightful that pleasure in playing alone quickly ceases. English upper-class education has always attributed an enormous moral importance to school games. To my mind, there is some exaggeration in the conventional British view, although I admit that games have certain important merits. They are good for health, provided they are not too expert; if exceptional skill is too much prized, the best players overdo it, while the others tend to lapse into spectators. They teach boys and girls to endure hurts without making a fuss, and to incur great fatigue cheerfully. But the other advantages which are claimed for them seem to me largely illusory. They are said to teach co-operation, but in fact they only teach it in its competitive form. This is the form required in war, not in industry or in the right kind of social relations. Science has made it technically possible to substitute co-operation for competition, both in economics and in international politics; at the same time it has made competition (in the form of war) much more dangerous than it used to be. For these reasons, it is more important than in former times to cultivate the idea of co-operative enterprises in which the 'enemy' is physical nature rather than competitive enterprises in which there are human victors and vanquished. I do not want to lay too much stress upon this consideration, because competitiveness is natural to man and must find some outlet, which can hardly be more innocent than games and athletic contests. This is a valid reason for not preventing games, but it is not a valid reason for exalting them into a leading position in the school curriculum. Let boys play because they like to do so, not because the authorities think games an antidote to what the Japanese call 'dangerous thoughts'.

BR OE 72–3

COMPETITIVE BUSINESS AND THE SOCIAL AIM

Parallel with and underlying most, if not all, the foregoing lies the general competitive business outlook and its resulting cultural effects. Particularly in this country has the spirit of competition for gain so permeated thinking and acting that many simply cannot understand any other state of affairs. To question 'the profit motive', for example, and propose instead some coöperative system seems, even to some eminent psychologists, like proposing to leave self altogether out of the motivation involved, as if the alternative to seeking profit at the expense of others must be an utter denial of self in favor of those others. These psychologists fail to see that coöperation implies common ends. As I share in the common efforts to attain these common ends, so I expect to share in the common output; but the motivation thus involved is neither selfishness nor altruism. That there are difficulties in getting coöperation started and in making it work is true, but to condemn the effort in advance as altruistic futility is in effect a refusal to face the reality where the actual difficulties are involved.

These considerations help to show the greatness of the task that confronts any who would urge our schools to more adequate work in the social realm. An economy run for personal gain, especially in a country where there have been such colossal opportunities for gain as in ours, so educates to its selfish individualistic outlook that unless something powerful happens to the contrary, the ordinary mind will be molded to this model. The ones who have profited most by the system believe, so tied up is the system they know with all they hold dear, that no good, only great harm, can come from allowing changes to creep in. This common attitude surrounds and permeates the thinking of the population in general, school people along with the rest. It is this prior permeation of the public mind with individualistic business ideas and the rights assumed to underlie them that explains the reactionary attitude of school boards and the aggressive character of the pressure groups considered above. It is the subtle permeation of this same spirit and attitude within the teaching profession itself which explains the easy success that conservative and reactionary forces have in keeping teaching so socially futile and innocuous.

BREAKING THE CIRCLE OF HURTFUL TRADITION

When a whole population seem caught in one all-inclusive climate of opinion, the question easily arises as to whether it is possible to break the spell, and if so how. It is again the problem of the 'vicious circle' referred to several times earlier: if tradition molds the rising generation to itself, how can progress ever come? The answer seems to lie, on the one hand, in the nature of thinking itself and, on the other hand, in the fact of inevitable change from which occasions arise that jar at least the more sensitive minds out of their thinking ruts. Of course, in so complex and shifting a civilization as ours, such a vicious circle could never be complete. The tradition never holds all equally in its grasp. Always are there some who have already been questioning, and their inquiries stimulate further inquiries.

In the matter of helping a people to think and so break this vicious circle of repetitive social tradition, teachers have advantages peculiar to them, best seen to be sure in university work but present also in secondary and elementary teaching. Under favorable conditions the work of teachers is unusually free from the distracting influences of the profit motive and from loyalty to formulations of belief as such. In fact in the university positive rewards, both in personal advancement and in professional reputation, await the man who picks successful flaws in hitherto accepted thinking, or perhaps even more raises a valid new question in a region where thought had been counted settled. Also, more than with most professions, the ideal of teaching is to cultivate in self and others the open-minded questioning attitude and to follow the resulting argument wherever it may lead, irrespective of any vested interests of doctrine or profit that may chance to be involved. And the tradition of academic freedom gives helpful immunity to the expression of views that selfish interests might otherwise wish emphatically to condemn. Most of all, the teaching function, from lowest to highest, affords the rare privilege of contact with young minds not yet closed by hardened habit or desire for selfish profit. Many of these minds are positively alert with curiosity to explore and learn, and vibrantly sensitive to the call of highest ideals. The call then, as we shall more fully discuss in later chapters, is upon the profession to live up to the possibilities thus open: to make the best possible selection of candidates, to give them the best possible preparation, to inspire them with the highest ideals of study and action, and to achieve for them the best possible working conditions. By such means can the teaching profession help the nation rise above mere tradition and learn instead to propose and weigh and choose according to the best attainable insight. In this way can we help break the vicious circle. Thus can thinking lead to progress.

But even so, to see the picture in full, there is another side. The surrounding tradition of business competition is, as already stated, very strong, especially upon those who must live in the business realm. Many a youth fired with zeal for high ideals in home or school has found outside of these a very different world. He hears that 'there is such a thing as being too honest,' that 'a man is not in business for his health,' that 'if a man expects to succeed he must not be afraid.' Such a one often, perhaps so far generally, ends in 'disillusionment.' The world of competitive profit has proved too strong for him. The cares of this world and the deceitfulness of riches have wrought his undoing.

Such is the situation teachers face as they attack the social problem. Within and without they are hindered and thwarted. Most powerful, perhaps, of all the forces to prevent the adequate pursuit of the social aim in our schools is the rival educative influence of the surrounding economic system run, as it is, competitively for private gain.

WHK TS 37–41

'The prize at the end introduces a breezy struggle for place.'

I shook my head.

'No competition! I won't have it. It makes the chap at the top of the class a prig, and gives the poor chap at the bottom an inferiority complex. No, we want to encourage not competition but co-operation. Competition leads naturally to another world war, as competition between British and American capital is doing now.'

Then Duncan floored me.

'And would you discourage football because it introduces the idea of competiton?' he asked.

'Of course not,' I replied.

'Then why discourage it in arithmetic?' he asked.

It was an arresting question, and I had to grope for an answer that would convince not only Duncan but myself. That every healthy boy likes to try his strength against his fellows is a fact that we cannot ignore. Mr Arthur Balfour's desire to beat his golfing partner and Jock Broon's desire to spit farther than Jake Tosh are fundamentally the same desire, the desire for self-assertion. And I see that the man who comes in last in the quarter-mile race is in the same position of inferiority as the boy who is always at the bottom of the class. Yet I condemn competition in school-work while I appreciate competition in games. Why?

I think I should leave it to the children. Obviously they like to compete in games and races, but they have no natural desire to compete in lessons. It appears that some things naturally lend themselves to competition—racing, boxing, billiards, jumping, football and so on. Other things do not encourage competition. Bernard Shaw and G. K. Chesterton do not compete in the output of books; Freud and Jung do not struggle to publish the record number of analysis cases; George Robey and Little Tich do not appear together on the stage of the Palladium and try to prove which is the funnier. Rivalry there always is, but it remains only rivalry until *The Daily Mail* offers a prize for the biggest cabbage or sweet-pea, and then competition seizes suburbia.

I should therefore leave the children to discover for themselves what interests lend themselves to competition, and what interests do not. I know beforehand that of their own accord they will not introduce it into school subjects. This is in accord with my views on the authority question. I insist that the teacher will impose nothing; that his task is to watch the children find their own solution. ASN DD 149–50

Curriculum

Laziness does not exist. What is called laziness is either lack of interest or lack of health. I have never yet seen a lazy child. A healthy child cannot be idle; he must be doing something all day long. But I have known a healthy lad who was known as a lazy fellow—at staff meetings when the mathematics teacher was reporting progress. Mathematics did not interest him, but the school code demanded that he should learn mathematics. I have seen a girl weep nightly over her geometry. Her mother wanted her to go to the university, but the girl's whole soul was artistic. I was delighted to hear lately that she failed in the London Matric. for the seventh time. Possibly the mother will now allow her to go on the stage that she longs for.

It is time that we were challenging the school's notion of work. It is taken for granted that every child should learn mathematics, history, geography, some science, a little art, literature. It is time that we realized that the average child is not interested in these subjects. I prove this with every new pupil. When told that the school is free, every new pupil cries: 'Hurrah! You won't catch me doing dull maths, and things' Every time.

A study of several free children will be of value.

Winifred, aged thirteen, came to me when the school was in Germany; came from a school with subjects. She told me that she hated all subjects, and shouted with joy when I told her she was free to do exactly as she liked.

'You don't even have to come to school if you don't want to,' I said.

She set herself out to have a good time, and she had—for a few weeks. Then I noticed that she was bored.

'Teach me something,' she said to me one day; 'I'm bored stiff.'

'Right ho!' I said cheerfully, 'what do you want to learn?'

'I don't know,' she said.

'And I don't either,' said I, and left her.

Months passed. Then she came to me again.

'I am going to pass the London Matric.,' she said, 'and I want lessons from you.'

Every morning she worked with me and other teachers—worked well. She confessed that the subjects did not interest her much, but the aim did interest her. Winifred found herself by being thrown on to herself.

ASN PC 118–20

Many separate controversies, in all of which other questions arise, are in part dependent upon our present question. Should boys learn mainly classics or mainly science? Among other considerations, one is that the classics are ornamental and science is useful. Should education as soon as possible become technical instruction for some trade or profession? Again the controversy between the useful and the ornamental is relevant, though not decisive. Should children be taught to enunciate correctly and to have pleasant manners, or are these merely relics of aristocracy? Is appreciation of art a thing of any value except in the artist? Should spelling be phonetic? All these and many other controversies are argued in part in terms of the controversy between the useful and the ornamental.

Nevertheless, I believe the whole controversy to be unreal. As soon as the terms are defined, it melts away. If we interpret 'useful' broadly and 'ornamental' narrowly, the one side has it; in the contrary interpretations, the other side has it. In the widest and most correct sense of the word, an activity is 'useful' when it has good results. And these results must be 'good' in some other sense than merely 'useful', or else we have no true definition. We cannot say that a useful activity is one which has useful results. The essence of what is 'useful' is that it ministers to some result which is not merely useful. Sometimes a long chain of results is necessary before the final result is reached which can be called simply 'good'. A plough is useful because it breaks up the ground. But breaking up the ground is not good on its own account; it is in turn merely useful because it enables seed to be sown. This is useful because it produces grain, which is useful because it produces bread, which is useful because it preserves life. But life must be capable of some intrinsic value: if life were merely useful as a means to other life, it would not be useful at all. Life may be good or bad according to circumstances; it may therefore also be useful, when it is a means to good life. Somewhere we must get beyond the chain of successive utilities, and find a peg from which the chain is to hang; if not, there is no real usefulness in any link of the chain. When 'useful' is defined in this way, there can be no question whether education should be useful. Of course it should, since the process of educating is a means to an end, not an end in itself. But that is not quite what the advocates of utility in education have in mind. What they are urging is that the *result* of education should be useful: put crudely, they would say that an educated man is a man who knows how to make machines. If we ask what is the use of machines, the answer is ultimately that they produce necessaries and comforts for the body—food, clothing, houses, etc. Thus we find that the advocate of utility, in the sense in which his view is questionable, is a man who attaches intrinsic value only to physical satisfaction: the 'useful', for him, is that which helps us to gratify the needs and desires of the body. When this is what is really meant, the advocate of utility is certainly in the wrong if he is enunciating an ultimate philosophy, though in a world where many people are starving he may be right as a politician, since the satisfaction of physical needs may be at the moment more urgent than anything else.

Much the same sort of dissection is necessary in considering the other side of this controversy. To call the other side 'ornamental' is, of course, to concede a point to the advocate of utility, since 'ornament' is understood to be more or less trivial. The epithet 'ornamental' is quite justified as applied to the traditional conception of a 'gentleman' or a 'lady'. The eighteenth century gentleman spoke with a refined accent, quoted the classics on appropriate occasions, dressed in the fashion, understood punctilio, and knew when a duel would advance his reputation. There is a man in *The Rape of the Lock,* who was

> of amber snuff-box justly vain,
> And the nice conduct of a clouded cane.

His education had been ornamental in the narrowest sense, and in our age few of us are rich enough to be content with his accomplishments. The ideal of an 'ornamental' education in the old sense is aristocratic: it presupposes a class with plenty of money and no need to work. Fine gentlemen and fine ladies are charming to contemplate in history; their memoirs and their country houses give us a certain kind of pleasure which we no longer provide for our posterity. But their excellences, even when real, were by no means supreme, and they were an incredibly expensive product; Hogarth's *Gin Lane* gives a vivid idea of the price that was paid for them. No one nowadays would advocate an ornamental education in this narrow sense.

But that is not the real issue. The real issue is: should we, in education, aim at filling the mind with knowledge which has direct practical utility, or should we try to give our pupils mental possessions which are good on their own account? It is useful to know that there are twelve inches in a foot, and three feet in a yard, but this knowledge has no intrinsic value; to those who live where the metric system is in use it is utterly worthless. To appreciate *Hamlet*, on the other hand, will not be much use in practical life, except in those rare cases where a man is called upon to kill his uncle; but it gives a man a mental possession which he would be sorry to be without, and makes him in some sense a more excellent human being. It is this latter sort of knowledge that is preferred by the man who argues that utility is not the sole aim of education.

There appear to be three different substantial issues wrapped up in the debate between advocates of a utilitarian education and their opponents. There is first a form of the debate between aristocrats and democrats, the former holding that the privileged class should be taught to employ its leisure in ways that are agreeable to itself, while the subordinate class should be taught to employ its labour in ways that are useful to others. The opposition of the democrats to this view tends to be somewhat confused: they dislike the teaching of what is useless to the aristocrat, and at the same time argue that the wage-earner's education should not be confined to what is useful. Thus we find a democratic opposition to the old-fashioned classical education in the public schools, combined with a democratic demand that working men should have opportunities for learning Latin and Greek. This attitude, even though it may imply some lack of theoretical clarity, is on the whole right in practice. The democrat does not wish to divide the community into two sections, one useful and one ornamental; he will therefore give more merely useful knowledge to the hitherto merely ornamental classes, and more merely delightful knowledge to the hitherto merely useful classes. But democracy, *per se*, does not decide the proportions in which these ingredients should be mixed.

The second issue is between men who aim only at material goods and men who care for mental delights. Most modern well-to-do Englishmen and Americans, if they were transported by magic into the age of Elizabeth, would wish themselves back in the modern world. The society of Shakespeare and Raleigh and Sir Philip Sydney, the exquisite music, the beauty of architecture, would not console them for the absence of bathrooms, tea and coffee, motor-cars, and other material comforts of which that age was ignorant. Such men, except in so far as they are influenced by conservative tradition, tend to think that the main purpose of education is to increase the number and variety of commodities produced. They may include medicine and hygiene, but they will not feel any enthusiasm for literature or art or philosophy. Undoubtedly such men have provided a great part of the driving force for the attack upon the classical curriculum established at the Renaissance.

I do not think it would be fair to meet this attitude by the mere assertion that mental goods are of more value than such as are purely physical. I believe this assertion to be true, but not the whole truth. For, while physical goods have no very high value, physical evils may be so bad as to outweigh a great deal of mental excellence. Starvation and disease, and the ever-present fear of them, have overshadowed the lives of the great majority of mankind since foresight first became possible. Most birds die of starvation, but they are happy when food is abundant, because they do not think about the future. Peasants who have survived a famine will be perpetually haunted by memory and apprehension.

BR OE 15–18

In the orthodox school, time-tabled by authority and motived in all academic work by individual penalties or reward, the only scope for group activity is in games; here there is some or much self-government; but in school-work authority dictates the whole, so that group comradeship in the classroom most easily fulfils itself by war with authority and by idleness; this is why boarding-schools so often become athletocracies. But where boys and girls are allowed self-government in school study, are encouraged (and not discouraged) to co-operate in their work, and have at least some rights over their own time-table, syllabus and methods of work, as well as some form of group rewards and group success, they can develop the same interest and enthusiasm in their work as in team games.

Each child brings to school the emotional make-up which his past environment has given him, varying affinities and repulsions in the unconscious mind for this or that school subject and for this or that type of personality in his teachers. In this respect the teacher's business is to make him natural again—not to make him good. The child is not an empty jug to be filled with knowledge; he is full already, full often of unconscious material which is faulty and which must be extracted and replaced by other things. Fear of punishment, and of loss of marks or of standing in class, and all kinds of imposed humiliation, will only exaggerate faults. The problem of schools is to re-awaken the play instinct (which is a social and co-operative instinct) in school-work, and to keep curiosity alive by the absence of institutionalism. Most teachers do not agree with this, and make the child do what he dislikes, as discipline. But a child only makes moral progress when he is happy. The true maxim runs that if we are happy we shall be good. If a child has interest in his work and is in each subject creating something for himself, he will go through with it. We may awaken interest by the stick, but not in the subject.

HL TPT 107–8

On the basis of these assumptions the old curriculum is *the requisite content of knowledge arranged systematically* (*logically*) *for progressive acquisition.*

This content was assigned for compulsory acquisition in the elementary and secondary schools, typically by 'lessons,' less often by lectures. Success of acquisition was tested, again typically, by daily recitations and at longer intervals by examinations; and success consisted, again typically, in ability to give back in words what had originally been assigned. The period primarily in mind for the actual functioning of the education was the life after school days were over.

As has been suggested in previous discussions, this older conception of education limits man and his educated life predominantly if not solely to intellect and counts memory as the primary means to intellect building. Behavior as such (beyond the behavior of proper study and recitation, obedience to teacher, and noninterference with the school process) had no place in this curriculum. Specifically, no consideration whatever was given to the conception of 'the whole child'; nor to the conception of cumulative concomitant learning, still less to the fact that these learnings are always in process, for good or ill. As against the various modern demands for the exercise of behavior traits in order to build them as traits into character, the assumption of this older intellectual memory type of curriculum was that if a child learned the right formulated statement, he would at the right time obey that statement and perform its content—a supposition everybody has always known to be in great measure fallacious if not entirely so.

The new curriculum outlook is so different from that just described that many brought up on the old, and familiar only with it, simply cannot understand the new. The way these people misconceive the new, and the absurd caricatures of it they readily accept and report, seem incredible. On bases discussed at length in previous chapters, the new curriculum makes at least six assumptions:

1. Education for the purpose here in mind is the effort of the adults in charge to guide the child's development and learning so that he may grow up to take his proper place in society and himself live the good life.

2. Each learns what he lives as he accepts it to live by, and he learns it in the degree that he accepts and lives it.

3. What one learns he builds, in corresponding degree, at once into character.

4. 'The whole child' is always involved, and many cumulative, concomitant learnings are always in process.

5. From these various considerations the school should be *a place of living*, living of the kind to help build the desirable all-round character to serve the all-round good life.

6. Teaching exists to cultivate this quality of living in those taught.

With these presuppositions before us, *the new curriculum becomes the total living of the child so far as the school can influence it or should take responsibility for developing it.*

By contrasting the two italicized definitions of the old and the new curriculums we see the essential difference. The old consists of a systematically arranged *content of formulated knowledge* which the learner is to acquire. The new consists of *the total living of the child* so far as the school can affect it, living of a kind to build the desired all-round character. The *old* seeks *knowledge* and vaguely hopes that somehow from this the good life will ultimately follow; the *new* seeks as its *immediate* aim the *highest and finest quality of living* that it can help effect, relying on the fact that if children do really live *this quality of life* they will in that degree build the *same quality of character*; for they do learn what they live and what is truly learned is therein built into character.

WHK PE 313–4

Since exams are not likely to be abolished for a long time, I have a practical proposition to make. It is this: that every teacher be compelled to sit Matric every time his students go forward for that exam. That would give them a fresh, if fearful orientation to the examination system. Personally I could not pass Matric. I might scrape through in English, maths, and German, but could not possibly pass in any other subjects. How salutary it would be for the children of a secondary school to learn that their maths master had failed in four subjects... including maths! I proposed to my own staff that we should all try the Matric, and was not much surprised at their consternation.

It is possible that the university trained teacher is more likely to overvalue exams than is the non-graduate teacher. In a university career one begins a journey marked by examination milestones, and the passing of each milestone gives the impression of progression, of achievement. The exams blind the student to the fact that the real permanent value of a university education is the social factor, the rubbing up against other students, the university debates and conversations.... The strong man throws a success behind him, and goes on to higher things, while the weakling fondles his little prize, and crows on the midden of his minor success. There is a lot of philosophy in the story of the old lady who asked Barrie what he was going to be. When he said: 'A writer,' she cried: 'What, and you an M.A.!'

Teachers should realize that success in life has little or nothing to do with trumpery little examinations. With the exception of university professors there is hardly a man of merit who has attained his eminence by passing exams. The great writers, the artists, the composers, the statesmen, the actors, the teachers ... their success is due to factors that no examination can touch. Examinations may be useful in the selection of the second-best in life, but that is about all they can do.

ASN PT 133-4

'For myself I wish to think of child and learning and subject-matter as all having a common denominator, as all belonging together in one single conception.'

'Your common-denominator, get-together, one-single-conception idea sounds good, but I can't think of any such. What have you to suggest?'

Experience as a unifying conception

'I like Dewey's, the conception of experience. The subject-matter of the curriculum is race experience, the picked winnings of the race, the best ways mankind has yet devised of meeting its problems.'

'That's all right for subject-matter, but where does the child come in? I thought we were to have a common denominator?'

'It is a common denominator. The child has experience, the race has experience. The child's experience is, of course, childish; but it is merely the small, the beginning, the germ; the fuller form we see in the race experience.'

'I get a glimmer of what you mean, but not all. Won't you elaborate?'

'Compare inch and hour with inch and mile. Inch and hour are, as was said, truly disparate. An inch is neither longer nor shorter than an hour nor yet equal to it. The two do not belong on the same scale. But with inch and mile it is different. An inch is shorter than a mile. If we think of a scale of length, an inch will belong on it, and so will a mile.'

'What are you talking about? I thought we were discussing experience as a common denominator for child and subject-matter.'

'So we are. Just wait. I say that on the scale of life or experience the child, like the inch on the mile, reaches but a small way. His ways of behaving are only beginnings, his language, for example, is limited and full of errors. The race experience, the best ways of behaving that man has yet devised, like the mile, reaches in comparison much longer. But—and this is my point—they both belong on the same scale. The best and wisest among us are in speech but doing better and wiser the same kind of thing the child is doing in his childish talk. There is no disparateness between the two. The greater is but the development to a higher degree of the less. Child-experience and race-experience are but earlier and later stages of the same thing.'

'As useful as is the term experience for your purpose, I think you used a phrase even better.'

'What was that?'

Ways-of-behaving as a unifying conception

'Ways-of-behaving. To me this is even a more obvious common denominator to child and subject-matter than is the notion of experience. The child is, if he is anything, a bundle of "ways-of-behaving". As you yourself said, the race-experience has preserved for us the best ways-of-behaving that have thus far been devised. Then child and subject-matter are both alike ways-of-behaving. The child's ways are small, crude, erring, perhaps, when we compare them with the best ways-of-behaving of the best among us; but they clearly belong on the same scale, as you have just brought out.'

'That sounds good, but let's look more closely. The combination $7 \times 8 = 56$ is subject-matter. How is it a way-of-behaving? Did you not too hastily include all subject-matter in your assertion?'

The way of behaving $7 \times 8 = 56$

'I think not. Consider a case where $7 \times 8 = 56$ actually belongs. I buy seven eight-cent stamps. I could pay for them separately, paying in at the stamp window eight cents seven distinct times—I mean in seven separate and distinct payments. That would be 7×8. But that is too much trouble. Thanks to our race experience (for many uncivilized tribes do not know so much arithmetic) instead of seven separate and distinct operations of paying eight cents each I make one paying operation of fifty-six cents. This race experience subject-matter way-of-behaving is much neater and more expeditious.'

'I had never thought of that before. And do all the things that we teach our children show the same thing? How about geography?'

Geography as ways-of-behaving

'It too, properly considered, consists of ways-of-behaving. I was in Detroit and learned to my regret that a certain train upon which I was relying did not, on account of the change to daylight saving time, get me into New York soon enough to meet an engagement. No other through train passing Detroit would do as well. Then came my geography. How about the Lake Shore road? Many trains between Chicago and New York pass that way, and the distance from Detroit down could not be great. There must surely be a road that would make the connection. Search disclosed such a connecting road with a satisfactory schedule of trains. A fast train to New York was caught and the engagement met. Here geographical knowledge actually meant a way-of-behaving. It told me where to look.'

'Would you be willing to say that all subject-matter in the curriculum really works this way?'

'I am quite willing to say that all *ought* to work this way; that anything which does not so work has no place in the curriculum.'

Ways-of-behaving and the curriculum

'This is one way then of critizing a curriculum?'

'Indeed it is, and trenchant criticism it gives too. Much curriculum content I fear could not stand it.'

'You would have to interpret behavior rather broadly, would you not, in order to include all desirable learnings under the head of ways-of-believing?'

'No more broadly than behavior properly extends. To me behavior is as broad as life; it specifically includes all ways of reacting in life to life situations. So far as I can see that will include all we need.'

'A moment ago you used this conception as a criterion for criticizing the curriculum. I am wondering if it is equally valuable as a criterion for judging learning.'

'What have you in mind?'

When learning has taken place

'I mean so as to decide whether a thing has been learned. We have said this in several different ways before. I should like now to say that nothing has been learned until it has been made over into an actual way-of-behaving. Much school learning seems to me to be merely for show purposes, chiefly for show on examination day. To me this is a degradation of the notion of learning, a prostitution of it. Nothing has been learned till it is there ready and disposed to serve as an actual way-of-behaving.'

'Wouldn't that condemn many schools and teachers?'

'I think it would, but it is no less valuable for all that. In fact I think our schools are often off the track. They seem not to know what they are about or why. If everybody saw that subject-matter is good only and because it furnishes a better way-of-behaving and that learning means acquiring actually that way-of-behaving—if every one saw these things, we should have, as we ought to have, a different kind of schools.'

'Does this have any bearing on education as a preparation for life?'

Education as the reconstruction of experience

'This conception helps us to understand one previously discussed, the continuous reconstruction of experience. To learn anything as a new way of behaving is of course to reconstruct experience. If we demand that the way-of-behaving be got only as it is immediately needed, we shall have the continuous remaking of experience; and this of course is life itself, living now—the opposite of education as a mere preparation for future living.'

'And you really mean that you wish everything the child learns to reappear soon as a new way of behaving? Everything—arithmetic, geography, history, spelling?'

'That is exactly what I mean. I should wish each thing to be learned when and because it was needed as a way-of-behaving right then and there. If it comes into the child's life because it is thus needed, I think it will sooner and more frequently and more vitally be called on to serve again in that child's life.'

'Do you mean there should be no variation from this, none whatever? Remember how many inferior teachers we have.'

'I told you what I should wish. In this world we often are compelled to take less than we wish.'

Group II

The role of the teacher

'What would you like to be when you grow up?' I have asked the question hundreds of times. Only once did a child reply: 'A teacher.' I had to send her away from my school later when she turned out to be mentally defective.

Yet children play schools and teachers, and one would suppose that to have command over many children would appeal to a child's sense of power. The superficial reason why children do not want to be teachers is that the teacher is associated with lessons, and the average child's ambition is to be free from lesson books for ever. The deeper reason is that the child longs to grow up, and vaguely he senses the truth that the teacher is the dunce who has to remain at school all his life. He is more: he is the Peter Pan who fears to face adult life. Every teacher has remained a little child.

Among teachers there are roughly two kinds of ungrown-ups: the kind that loves being a child, and the kind that hates his inability to grow up. The former is what we call 'the born teacher': the latter is the hateful disciplinarian. The born teacher is not a problem: he loves his work and he loves children, and children love him. But he should be pensioned off about the early forties because, when he arrives at the stage when play is an effort to him, he is apt to become a pessimist with a mechanical smile.

The disciplinarian teacher should of course be pensioned off before he leaves the training college. He is dangerous and damned from the word go. Psychologically he is at the same stage as the bully of Class IV, but he is a bully who is in the position of being winner in every scrap. The born teacher is the Peter Pan of love: the disciplinarian the Peter Pan of power. Love is the sun that warms children, but power is the night that terrorises them....

The word education means literally drawing out, and it has

often been said that the successful teacher is he or she who can most easily draw out from the child what he knows. It is a limited and, in a manner, a wrong definition, just as wrong as the idea that a good teacher is one who puts things into a child. A good teacher does not draw out: he gives out, and what he gives out is love. And by love I mean approval, or if you like friendliness, good nature. The good teacher not only understands the child: he approves of the child. The ability to teach a subject is of minor importance: the one criterion applicable to any teacher is . . . Do children fear him? If they do he is a bad teacher, even though he has 100 per cent of passes every year. If he is respected by his pupils he is a failure, for respect implies fear. I have said often and often that if a child cannot address his teacher as a silly ass the teacher is a danger.

ASN PT 9–11

The teacher should not be expected to flatter the prejudices either of the mob or of officials. His professional virtue should consist in a readiness to do justice to all sides, and in an endeavour to rise above controversy into a region of dispassionate scientific investigation. If there are people to whom the results of his investigation are inconvenient, he should be protected against their resentment, unless it can be shown that he has lent himself to dishonest propaganda by the dissemination of demonstrable untruths.

The function of the teacher, however, is not merely to mitigate the heat of current controversies. He has more positive tasks to perform, and he cannot be a great teacher unless he is inspired by a wish to perform these tasks. Teachers are more than any other class the guardians of civilization. They should be intimately aware of what civilization is, and desirous of imparting a civilized attitude to their pupils. We are thus brought to the question: what constitutes a civilized community?

This question would very commonly be answered by pointing to merely material tests. A country is civilized if it has much machinery, many motor cars, many bathrooms, and a great deal of rapid locomotion. To these things, in my opinion, most modern men attach much too much importance. Civilization, in the more important sense, is a thing of the mind, not of material adjuncts to the physical side of living. It is a matter partly of knowledge, partly of emotion. So far as knowledge is concerned, a man should be aware of the minuteness of himself and his immediate environment in relation to the world in time and space. He should see his own country not *only* as home, but as one among the countries of the world, all with an equal right to live and think and feel. He should see his own age in relation to the past and the future, and be aware that its own controversies will seem as strange to future ages as those of the past seem to us now. Taking an even wider view, he should be conscious of the vastness of geological epochs and astronomical abysses; but he should be aware of all this, not as a weight to crush the individual human spirit, but as a vast panorama which enlarges the mind that contemplates it. On the side of the emotions, a very similar enlargement from the purely personal is needed if a man is to be truly civilized. Men pass from birth to death, sometimes happy, sometimes unhappy; sometimes generous, sometimes grasping and petty; sometimes heroic, sometimes cowardly and servile. To the man who views the procession as a whole, certain things stand out as worthy of admiration. Some men have been inspired by love of mankind; some by supreme intellect have helped us to understand the world in which we live; and some by exceptional sensitiveness have created beauty. These men have produced something of positive good to outweigh the long record of cruelty, oppression, and superstition. These men have done what lay in their power to make human life a better thing than the brief turbulence of savages. The civilized man, where he cannot admire, will aim rather at understanding than at reprobating. He will seek rather to discover and remove the impersonal causes of evil than to hate the men who are in its grip. All this should be in the mind and heart of the teacher, and if it is in his mind and heart he will convey it in his teaching to the young who are in his care.

No man can be a good teacher unless he has feelings of warm affection towards his pupils and a genuine desire to impart to them what he himself believes to be of value. This is not the attitude of the propagandist. To the propagandist his pupils are potential soldiers in an army. They are to serve purposes that lie outside their own lives, not in the sense in which every generous purpose transcends self, but in the sense of ministering to unjust privilege or to despotic power. The propagandist does not desire that his pupils should survey the world and freely choose a purpose which to them appears of value. He desires, like a topiarian artist, that their growth shall be trained and twisted to suit the gardener's purpose. And in thwarting their natural growth he is apt to destroy in them all generous vigour, replacing it by envy, destructiveness, and cruelty. There is no need for men to be cruel; on the contrary, I am persuaded that most cruelty results from thwarting in early years, above all from thwarting what is good.

BR UE 152–4

The next step will be to choose the most promising of these suggestions. The teacher will have in mind (i) possible values to be sought (as found in his own 'map' of values); (ii) the more promising lines of activity apparently open to the class; and (iii) some conception of the class interests and aptitudes (as disclosed by its previous record). Pupils and teachers will together consider the several items on the list, the teacher aiming to get from the class as intelligent and responsible discussion as possible. To meet the needs of the situation the activity chosen should (i) rank high in class interest; (ii) be difficult enough to challenge the best efforts of the pupils, but not so difficult as to threaten discouragement; (iii) rank high in promising valuable items on the 'map' of values, items that fit well with the past and lead well into the future. Of these requirements, the first, the presence of active interest, is a necessary condition, but not of itself a sufficient condition. Granted a reasonably high interest and challenge, the teacher will seek the third factor, the highest possible promise of values. Preferably, however, it will be the pupils who finally choose; for their cordial commitment is necessary, particularly at first, for any good hope of success.

4. This matter of commitment is so important as to demand emphasis. The individual pupil inevitably will learn in the degree that he himself accepts the activity or the enterprise or the experience undertaken. The teacher will accordingly work, through the process of group discussion and choice, to get the individual learners and the class as a whole committed as wholeheartedly as possible to the activity chosen.

5. In connection with what has just been said, almost a variant of its outworking, the teacher will from start to finish encourage in the pupils as high a degree of self-directed responsible acting on

thinking as it is possible to get. To feel one's self acting responsibly and so helping to create what is being done, and to do this in a way to deserve respect from others, is one of the very keenest of satisfactions; it almost certainly means strong commitment, and the learning that goes on in connection with it is likely to be very strong.

6. As the correlative of the last two items, learner commitment and responsible learner creating, the teacher's task becomes, as previously stated, primarily that of guidance. The teacher will, to be sure, help the individual learner or the class as may prove necessary, but always so as to help the learners to help themselves. It is what pupils do of themselves that brings the best learning results, both in direct learning and in concomitant learnings. We can thus say, paradoxically, that the teacher's aim is to give as little help as possible, that is, to give the least degree of direct help consistent with the best personal work on the part of the pupils. (Even so the modern teacher works harder and continually helps pupils more than did the old type of teacher.)

7. In accordance with the foregoing, the teacher will as well as possible help the learners at each stage of the effort: (i) to initiate the activity (to form or choose the purpose); (ii) to plan how to carry the activity forward; (iii) to execute the plan; (iv) to evaluate progress during the activity and the result at the end. While all this is going forward the teacher will also (v) encourage the learners to think up and note suggestions or new leads for other and further work; (vi) help them to formulate these suggestions both for clarification of thinking and for later recall and possible use (perhaps writing them in a book or on the board for future reference); (vii) help pupils criticize their thinking en route or at the close, as may seem wise; and finally (viii) look back over the whole process to pick up and fix important kinds of learning involved as well as draw lessons for the future from both successes and failures.

WHK PE 306–7

The paper read by Lane to the Little Commonwealth Committee after the Rawlinson Enquiry (*22nd June, 1918*).

The distressing situation, in which you and all the others who have supported the Little Commonwealth during the past five years, now find themselves can only be tolerated by a conviction of the sincerity of those to whom you have entrusted your work, and a knowledge that the circumstances that have brought about the subject-matter of this meeting are the results of errors, frankly admitted, rather than carelessness or lack of interest in behalf of the children under your care.

I beg of you, if it is possible under the circumstances, to place yourselves now in the position of the physician rather than that of the coroner; to conduct a diagnosis of the patient's ailments rather than a post-mortem examination of his remains.

I wish, at the very outset, to admit that the present position of this committee is due to a serious professional error on my part; an error which I will be grateful to you for examining in its proper relation to the content of your diagnosis.

The task which I will undertake is an exceedingly difficult one. The psychological principles upon which the Commonwealth has been built are comparatively new to the educational world. They involve the psychology not only of delinquent boys and girls but of insane persons and normal people as well. Any examination, then, of the psychological theories of the Commonwealth, if thorough enough to be convincing, must touch upon those feelings and instincts which are the base and foundation of morality and ethics and of social and spiritual consciousness as well; instincts and feelings which are common to every human being whether criminal, insane, normal or brilliantly successful in life. Could it be possible for you to explore this new area in psychological research as a detached intellect, with only reason and logic operative in reaching your conclusion, my task and yours would be infinitely easier. But your own deepest feelings and prejudices will probably intrude upon those conclusions both for and against, as the case may be, your arrival at a complete and detailed understanding of my error and of your responsibility for the future of your school.

Prof. Freud conducted his research in the interests of those persons who came under his care as a physician specializing in the treatment of mental diseases. The relief he and his students and followers have afforded to unfortunate humanity suffering from various forms of insanity is incalculable. Some of the almost instantaneous cures his science has affected seem almost miraculous. Indeed, it is the science and its techniques developed by Freud that is applied in the treatment of that most pitiable of all the misfortunes of the soldier known as shell-shock with such remarkable results. Still however the deep-rooted and harsh prejudice against the Freudian theory persists.

Now I have had the presumption to undertake to employ Freud's technique for the purposes of education, by a reverse process. He unravels the tangles in an unhappy and fruitless life, making the insane sane. I have tried to use his technique in education, in the building up of lives of joy and usefulness. He corrects insanity, I am trying to create sanity. He found that the great majority of his patients developed the symptoms of their several mental diseases during adolescence. It is obvious that in the treatment of my pupils I should find many evidences of mental abnormality, more or less developed, since I am dealing with persons well advanced in adolescence and who at the same time are delinquents. I must therefore use the Freudian technique in psychology in helping nearly every one of my pupils, in both directions, viz: to remove already formed obsessions and phobias from their paths, and then in a reverse process, re-educating and re-building.

So far as I am aware, no other teacher has attempted to employ the Freudian methods systematically in any school, I have not had the benefit of any other teacher's experience in a parallel effort. A recently published book by Oskar Pfister of Zurich, a pastor, is the first instance that has come to my notice of any other attempt to employ psycho-analysis for the improvement of normal people. Even Pfister has apparently not used the new psychology as an aid in academic education or the development of the social instincts that underlie these qualities that make for good citizenship.

If, then, I may assume that I am a pioneer in psycho-analytic education, may I not also assume the privilege of stating the premise upon which the technique of psycho-analysis rests for the purpose of practical application to education.

The psycho-analyst, physician, or teacher must exercise two distinct but related functions. First, he must diagnose his patients' difficulties. He, with the co-operation of his patient, explores the unconscious mind, analyses the tendencies of the libido, dissolves complexes or repressed wishes that are inacceptable to consciousness by re-awakening memory, discovers the particular manner in which each complex affects conduct and conscious effort, and educates the patient as to the thousand and one inclinations of his libido. This process is merely the diagnosis.

The second function or treatment consists in a process of redirecting the libido, now freed from unwholesome or futile pursuits, into channels of activity that will serve the life-purposes of the conscious mind. This function is called Sublimation. As the word implies, the process is simply the elevation of the interests of the unconscious to the higher emotions and efforts that will serve the purpose of realization of the ethical and moral ideals of the conscious mind.

The sublimation process is education, pure and simple. Every teacher, even those who have never heard of psycho-analysis, is attempting the sublimation of his pupil's libido. But the chief characteristic of the libido being, as it is, a tendency to attach its cravings to an instinctive and un-moral interest in the life-cycle, the non-analytic teacher, being unaware of the already existing attachments of the libido is, by his method, producing a titanic unconscious conflict in his pupil. This conflict between the moral conscious motive and the unconscious, instinctive cravings of the libido is the source of nine-tenths of the unhappiness and inefficiency in the world. If you at this moment recall incidents of forgetfulness in your own experience you will notice that you only forget those things in which there is an element of conscious distaste. If you suffer from procrastination you will find by self-analysis that you only put off doing those things that you consciously dislike doing. If a pupil dislikes history he is never good at that subject, and there is a definite origin for his dislike in the Unconscious. His failure is due to unconscious conflict. Every unconscious conflict in all persons—and no person is without them—has pathological effects. Whatever degree of inefficiency we, each of us, recognize in ourselves is due to unconscious conflict. The libido needs to be detached from some instinctive anti-social activity and re-directed toward the conscious life-purpose.

Does your boy hate arithmetic? He can be made to love it by analytic pedagogy. Is he rude and ungracious? It is conflict easily removable. Is he purposely annoying? He is suffering from an inferiority complex. His libido can be detached from its unwholesome goal. Does he bite his nails? Fidget in his chair? Has he an obsession for drumming with his fingers? Sucking the end of his pen? Teasing his brother or sister? Whistling? Throwing stones? Does he have a morbid interest in ghostly sights? Is he afraid of ghosts, burglars or goblins? All these things and thousands of others are inevitably the manifestations or unconscious conflicts raging within him and as such can be dealt with certainly and scientifically by analysis.

That period of life called by Ferrier 'The Criminal Age' by schoolmasters 'the storm Period', by policemen a less polite but more expressive term—the period between the ages of eleven and eighteen is full of unconscious conflict. The libido is struggling against moral and social consciousness. The intensity of the struggle is determined by the degree of moral resistance that must be overcome by the libido in its craving for gratification.

If the moral consciousness is weak and artificial—not based upon experienced truths—conscious and but slightly resisted sexual perversion, purposeful lying, etc., etc., ensue.

If the social consciousness is founded upon an artificial base, such at the constant suppression of activity by the parent or teacher furnishes, obsessional thieving, hatred of parents or teachers, cruelty in its various forms, etc., etc., are the characteristics of conduct. The conflict is not intense—the libido speaks with a direct and but slightly disguised voice.

If on the other hand the moral consciousness is strong and the libido not already attached to other wholesome and love stimulating activities, the conflict between the instinctive craving and the conscious moral will is intense. The libido must disguise its effect in the conscious mind. The result is hypocrisy, fixation of libido upon the parent or obsessional love with hysterical symptoms, penuriousness, snobbery, priggishness, over-fastidiousness, sentimentality, competitivenes, etc., etc.

Masochism or self-torment, and sadism or obsessional cruelty to others is a not unusual form in which the libido escapes detection and eludes the vigilance of a strong conscious sex-morality. Self-destruction and murderous tendencies are developments of masochism and sadism and are invariably the results of the unconscious conflicts that rage within us all through life, but most intensely during puberty and adolescence. These and other fruitful sources of life-long misery may be removed from the paths of our boys and girls by the introduction into our schemes of education of a scientific psychological basis for the moral and ethical structure we wish to erect.

The unhappy circumstances that brought about the necessity for this meeting today are the result of unconscious conflicts and sex perversities of citizens of the Commonwealth. One of my accusers is a pronounced sadist who has an obsessional fondness for Charlie Chaplin and his brutal comedy; the other is a masochist. These two mental diseases are more prevalent in the Commonwealth than in any other community which I have known. It is not difficult to account for this in the light of psycho-analytic knowledge as follows:

The conscious moral principles instilled deeply into the minds of the citizens of the Commonwealth by our form of self-government is so intense and so surely based upon logic and reason and experience that the libido which is definitely directed toward erotic or love objects, by the co-educational features of our school, must assume the deepest disguise in its power in order to evade the censor and affect the consciousness of the individual. Hence the prevalence of masochism or self-accusation in the Commonwealth.

These unfortunate incidents, in spite of the painful position in which we are all placed have the effect, in my own mind, of re-affirming my confidence in self-government, co-education and 'Commonwealth' principles in education.

Let me explain this paradox. It is at this point that I wish you to examine the error on my part that is responsible for the incidents that have given you so much anxiety during the past six months.

The employment of a technical term to scientifically represent the normal relation between parent and child, teacher and pupil, physician and patient, pastor and parishioner, employer and employee—the use of the word 'transference' instead of the word we use in our everyday thoughts—love, confidence, respect, trust, loyalty, puts many unthoughtful people off. It associates, wrongfully, with hypnotism or some form of surrender of will to another. The psychological relation between analyst and patient is the extreme opposite of hypnotism.

The patient transfers to his analyst, temporarily, as being for the moment the nearest person he can love, only that which belongs to the parent or the pupil's vocation, as the case may be according to his age and degree of independence.

The non-analytic teacher must depend upon chance or accident to dissolve the transference. His pupil is the victim of circumstances in so far as his libido will attach itself to some interest or other, irrespective of morals or success in life. For the libido is unmoral until brought under the control of the consciousness.

The analytic teacher positively indicates the object or pursuit to the re-transferred libido. If the teacher refuses to accept the transference (love) of his pupil's libido, it may take a negative form and become hate. The transference is, however, inevitable.

I must make this point clear, even at the risk of boring you, for it is the critical point in analytic education, and the point at which my disastrous error occurred.

Those of you who have observed Montessori classes at work will have noticed that different teachers obtain different results in applying the same system. One teacher's class loves certain tasks and neglects others. Another teacher secures excellent results in the tasks that the pupils of the other teacher fail in, etc. An analysis of the teacher would explain the mystery in terms of transference. The teacher, herself, has interest in the things her pupils are successful in, and lacks interest in the activities which her pupils do poorly. The analysed teacher would then discover the cause of her own pupil's failure, and by having knowledge in herself of her own unconscious dislike of those activities, would be able to dissolve that dislike and secure the transference of the child's libido to the hitherto disliked work.

I say the teacher would be able to dissolve her unconscious dislike for certain activities. Let me affirm this scientifically, as follows: Every teacher 'transfers' parental love to his or her pupil. The teachers libido is (or should be) attached to the pupil, but not necessarily to the task the pupil is performing. Therefore, having secured conscious knowledge, through analysis, of her unconscious dislike of the distasteful work, it disappears at once because she sees the reflection of that dislike in her pupil.

I would go a step farther still. The teacher who does not love the subjects he is teaching will find his lack of love reflected in his pupil's lack of accomplishment. Any 'analysed' teacher may 'sublimate' to love any subject that he thinks will benefit his 'first love' his pupil. Ergo:

no one should teach who has not been himself analysed and through the process gained that true psychological insight which produces the 'Art of Teaching'.

Now I may confess my error and ask your forgiveness on a sound basis with all the elements exposed to view.

When, five years ago, I undertook the task of organizing the Commonwealth I was familiar to some extent with the theories and techniques of psycho-analysis. I have always, up to a few weeks ago, felt a strong distaste for the responsibilities involved in making known to my pupils' conscious minds the fact of the transference of their libido to me as the 'nearest parents'. I knew that this transference was inevitable but I shrank from the responsibilities entailed by their consciousness of it. I devised a method of avoiding that responsibility that, until a few weeks ago, I sincerely believed in. The method was this: by allowing my pupils to create a community of their own, frame their own laws, administer their own courts, they being independent of their own parents' assistance through the wages scheme of the Commonwealth, I sought to secure transference from their own parents direct to their community without any intermediary in myself. (This seemed reasonable. The soldier transfers from his wife and children to his country.) I felt that by making myself a member of the community on equal terms with themselves, that whatever transference was made to me, personally, would be in their conscious minds an added love for their community. I felt that self-analysis by means of group criticism of each other as in the courts would become automatic. I hoped that the absence of adult and dogmatic moral authority would result in a minimizing of unconscious conflicts in the individual, and that the libido of each citizen would become firmly attached to the vocational, social and spiritual, interests of the Commonwealth. I hoped and confidently expected that the Commonwealth would become the criterion of other schools as the result of its scientific use of all the powers of the mind. I confidently expected that the experiment would develop a scheme by which other schools might be similarly organized even though the heads were not psychologists. The technique of psycho-analysis is so difficult of mastery, the study of psychology occupies so much time and concentration, that I felt the great need of devising some method of bringing about mind-analysis automatically.

The events of the past six months have convinced me of the futility of trying to cut psychological corners in educational schemes. I now gladly abandon my beautiful scheme after five years' faithful adherence to it. Mr Rawlinson has completely dissolved my complex. I now see clearly that the adolescent must still have a parent-substitute to accept his libido temporarily for purposes of dissolving complexes and conflicts, before that libido can be transferred to the community in which he lives. The progress of the exalted craving that eventually brings about the completion of the life-cycle cannot be hurried. The adolescent is still a child.

This is the point at which my error occurred—the error that will account, reasonably, for a great many of the disappointments we have had in the citizens who have failed to achieve the standard of usefulness and character we had set for them.

I have been accused by my friends of 'genius' for dealing with children. It may now be seen, in the light of the psychological principles I have so imperfectly explained to you, that my relationship with my charges is logical, reasonable and scientific. Underlying the logic and reason and science is a libido that is firmly attached to the higher interests and happiness of all the citizens of the Commonwealth.

I and you and our boys and girls have suffered, in different degrees of suffering, because of my error but I hope that that error will not include, as one of its results, the abandonment of a sincere, although imperfect, attempt to employ the whole of the mind, instinctive as well as conscious, in the purposes for which the education of our children is undertaken.

HL in WDW 254–5, 261–7

The class teacher may reply: It isn't my job to deal with the inner life of the child. I am paid for teaching the little devil arithmetic. Yes, but whose job is it then? Suppose Tommy has phobias: suppose he has inordinate death fears or wishes: suppose he is miserably unhappy. If the teacher cannot help him who can? Not his parents, not the clergyman, not the local doctor. If he steals, your punishment will make him worse, for he is seeking love and you will give him hate. If you punish him for bullying he will retain his bullying attitude longer than he would have done because he is reinforced by the added knowledge that you are also a bully.

It is the teacher's job to be the soul doctor to the child, to every child in the classroom. This of course cannot be carried out if the teacher attempts to serve God and Mammon, to be the soul doctor and the sergeant-major at one and the same time. In my own work I have this difficulty. New children identify me for a long time with their former teachers, and if these teachers have been strict disciplinarians, I find that it takes me weeks and often months to get into touch with the child. Only when they feel that I am not an authority do they come to me with their soul troubles. When children come young enough, at three to seven, they never show this hate and fear of authority, but then when they come so young they seldom need much in the way of soul-doctoring.

Teachers have often said to me: 'It's all very well for you. You have been at the job for years, but although I want to help kids sometimes, I simply don't know how to begin. I don't know enough about psychology.'

But neither do I. I may know more than many teachers because I have concentrated on the subject for years, but if a child has night terrors I have to begin at the beginning and slowly try to find out, by what the child says, what the possible cause is. Sometimes I succeed: sometimes I fail. In the latter case the trouble often disappears mysteriously without the root having been discovered. The cure is in all likelihood due to the comfort the child finds in getting an adult to side with it and comfort it.

I really do not think that a training in psychology is so necessary as a sympathetic attitude. It must be a non-moral attitude. If a child told you it had murdered its grandmother you would have to receive the news with as much emotion as you would receive the news that the child had got a new teddy bear. It would depend on your attitude to your own grandmother anyway.

A moral attitude judges and condemns. In a teacher such an attitude is fatal. Even if the teacher hides it with a smile or a look of indifference the child feels it, for he has so uncanny a gift of seeing behind the adult's mask.

ASN PT 59–60

These considerations bring us to the province of psycho-analysis. There is much in the detail of psycho-analysis which I find fantastic, and not supported by adequate evidence. But the general method appears to me very important, and essential to the creation of right methods of moral training. The importance which many psycho-analysts attach to early infancy appears to me exaggerated; they sometimes talk as if character were irrevocably fixed by the time a child is three years old. This, I am sure, is not the case. But the fault is a fault on the right side. Infant psychology was neglected in the past; indeed, the intellectualist methods in vogue made it almost impossible. Take such a matter as sleep. All mothers wish their children to sleep, because it is both healthy and convenient when they do. They had developed a certain technique: rocking the cradle and singing lullabies. It was left for males, who investigated the matter scientifically, to discover that this technique is ideally wrong, for though it is likely to succeed on any given day, it creates bad habits. Every child loves to be made a fuss of, because its sense of self-importance is gratified. If it finds that by not sleeping it secures attention, it will soon learn to adopt this method. The result is equally damaging to health and character. The great thing here is the formation of habit: the association of the cot with sleep. If this association has been adequately produced the child will not lie awake unless it is ill or in pain. But the production of the association requires a certain amount of discipline; it is not to be achieved by mere indulgence, since that causes pleasurable associations with lying awake. Similar considerations apply to the formation of other good and bad habits. This whole study is still in its infancy, but its importance is already very great, and almost sure to become greater. It is clear that education of character must begin at birth, and requires a reversal of much of the practice of nurses and ignorant mothers. It is also clear that definite instruction can begin earlier than was formerly thought, because it can be made pleasant and no strain upon the infant's powers of attention. In both these respects educational theory has been radically transformed in recent years, with beneficient effects which are likely to become more and more evident as the years go by. Accordingly I shall begin, in what follows, with a fairly detailed consideration of the training of character in infancy, before discussing the instruction to be given in later years.

BR OE 26–7

Love

There seems to have been a tacit implication in the speaker's attack on the theory of original sin, that hate is *something foreign to human nature. Is hate not part of our instinctive make-up? Can't we admit hate without repressing it, and direct it to such things as exploitation?*

The end of the question suggests an amiable cynic. Freud holds that hate comes first, that love is a later development. I cannot follow the argument. I have never seen any signs of hate in a new-born infant. My belief in original virtue arises from my observation of children who hate. When they are loved they drop their hate. It is true that small children bicker with each other in their endeavours to find power. But the bickering is only a serious affair when the children are being made to hate themselves by being moralized to by adults. The bickering is not hate. Hate is love transformed, rather it is thwarted love. It is not the opposite of love, for the opposite of love is obviously indifference. Thus small children are much more likely to quarrel with their brothers and sisters than with outside children, for in the home there is an emotional atmosphere which is allied to love. Hate in a child arises when he finds that he is not getting enough love from his parents. I have seen many a young hater come to Summerhill biting and scratching, but in six months our haters become social lovable characters. I am forced to conclude that hate is not a clear instinct; it must be acquired. How it comes to be acquired is the big mystery of life. If the child is born good why then do we have warmakers and kill-joys and Calvinistic haters of the body? What makes the adult man treat his fellows with cruelty? Why does a respectable magistrate order boys to be flogged?

ASN TDS 153–4

All organic life may be represented as a wish. Man, the highest form of life, is in himself the product of the cumulative wishes of all organic life in past ages. Man is the embodiment of the master-wish for perfection of the universe, and is therefore essentially good. The motive-power of goodness is love, and love is compulsory. If a man does not love mankind and the universe, he is not true to his nature. Man does not choose to love; he must love.

If he hates, his behaviour is untrue to himself, to mankind and to the universe, but the energy is still love, for his act of hatred is love perverted. The hateful act is destructive of the man's self, and also of the happiness and welfare of mankind, thus retarding the perfection of the universe. It is wholly unnatural.

The loving act is hopeful behaviour, the hateful act is fearful behaviour. But he who serves his fellow-man by effort of will is making love a virtue. Love is not a virtue; it is natural to mankind.

According to his conception of authority, man will either progress toward perfection, obeying the master-wish, or regress to the primitive. The only true authority is love, and the only true discipline is founded upon hope. The authority that is based upon force will transform love into hatred and hope into fear.

If a man's love be not extended to all mankind and all communities, he cannot be completely happy; for love is dynamic and universal.

HL TPT 177

Indeed my chief and perhaps only virtue is patience. In my therapy with Reich he kept telling me that I was repressing my hate, trying to be too much of a Christlike person. It may be, but I find it difficult to hate. They say that if you cannot hate you cannot love. Maybe. I have never been able to give out what might be called personal love to children, and certainly never sentimental love. The word sentimental is difficult of definition; I call it giving a swan emotion to a goose. Thus I have never had favourites in the school. Sure I have liked some children better than others, yet have always managed to keep from betraying it. Possibly the success of Summerhill has been in part due to the feeling that the children had that they were all Jock Tamson's bairns, all treated alike and treated with respect. I fear the existence in any school of a sentimental attitude to the pupils; it is so easy to make your geese swans, to see a Picasso in a child who can splash colour about.

It is all a matter of awareness. Without awareness you cannot be objective. Put it this way: if a man does not know he has a strong mother complex he will have a blind eye to mother complexes in his pupils. Being aware means being free from prejudices, from infantile attitudes, rather as free as possible, for who can ever get free of early conditionings?

ASN FC 11

Many readers may think that I have hitherto unaccountably neglected affection, which is, in some sense, the essence of a good character. I hold that love and knowledge are the two main requisites for right action, yet, in dealing with moral education, I have hitherto said nothing about love. My reason has been that the right sort of love should be the natural fruit resulting from the proper treatment of the growing child, rather than something consciously aimed at throughout the various stages. We have to be clear as to the kind of affection to be desired, and as to the disposition appropriate to different ages. From ten or twelve years old until puberty a boy is apt to be very destitute of affection, and there is nothing to be gained by trying to force his nature. Throughout youth there is less occasion for sympathy than in adult life, both because there is less power of giving effective expression to it, and because a young person has to think of his or her own training for life, largely to the exclusion of other people's interests. For these reasons we should be more concerned to produce sympathetic and affectionate adults than to force a precocious development of these qualities in early years. Our problems in the education of character, is a scientific one, belonging to what may be called psychological dynamics. Love cannot exist as a duty: to tell a child that it *ought* to love its parents and its brothers and sisters is utterly useless, if not worse. Parents who wish to be loved must behave so as to elicit love, and must try to give to their children those physical and mental characteristics which produce expansive affections.

Not only must children not be commanded to love their parents, but nothing must be done which has this result as its object. Parental affection, at its best, differs from sex love in this respect. It is of essence of sex love to seek a response, as is natural, since, without a response, it cannot fulfil its biological function. But it is not of the essence of parental love to seek a purpose.

BR OE 104

Since the heart the work of the profession of education is to guide the educative process, the preparation of the educator proceeds along two correlative lines. He must understand, on the one hand, the individual life process and how learning is essential in it to its continuous upbuilding; and, on the other hand, the social process and how education is essential in it also to its continuous up-building. And the educator must be devoted to his work. No mere hireling will suffice. He must love to work with others and help them grow. . . .

WHK GF 262

Ideas on learning and development

The degree of difficulty in the control of toys is important in the evolution of mental power. First, give a small ball that the child can hold in one hand; then go on to a larger one, which requires both hands to grasp it, so that both hemispheres of the brain are employed, and get their proper exercise and development. This is particularly important if the child shows a tendency to use one hand only, as is not uncommon. All differences and novelty of sound, colour, surface or weight will draw interest into new and wider fields. The basis of a knowledge of physics, mathematics, and dynamics may be laid at this age by giving the child balls and toys of different weights, as of celluloid, rubber, and wood, so that one, when dropped, makes a more perceptible bump on the knees than another. The child will not reason about it, but will unconsciously learn a good deal about the density of materials. If the first contact with this kind of knowledge is pleasant, then when a child comes to a physics laboratory at twelve or fourteen, he will find a sense of enjoyment and interest. Much can be done to lay foundations for the schoolmaster by giving the child opportunities for the pleasant exercise of power.

HL TPT 147

The child always wants to be in a group, but only in order to have someone to show off to. It has no real idea of co-operation; giving in to others is merely the price to be paid for getting an audience; the child must agree to certain rules in order to obtain a chance of self-assertion. Thus the child only fields at cricket because otherwise it will get no turn to bat. It had not the idea of the good of the team.

A child of seven therefore requires a group of children to play with, in order to develop his social instincts in the form which they then have. The group should not consist of his brothers and sisters, for towards them he will always have some attitude of 'elder' or 'younger.' In order that he may become truly social in adult life, he must at the age of self-assertion acquire by competition the nucleus of social sense. Watching the spontaneous organizations of children at this age in slum districts, where alone children are to be seen perfectly natural, free from authority, and thrown on their own resources, we see that in a street containing anything from twenty to a hundred boys and girls, the children will always organize into small groups, never a mob. The group will never be less than three and not more than seven or eight—the right size to give them the values they are seeking in their fantasies; so it seems that the proper-sized group should number five to eight.

HL TPT 95

Seeing that his inferiority to other people is normal, not pathological, its compensation in fantasy is also normal and not pathological. His games do not take up time which might be more profitably spent in other ways: if all his hours were given over to serious pursuits, he would soon become a nervous wreck. An adult who indulges in dreams may be told to exert himself in order to realize them; but a child cannot yet realize dreams which it is right that he should have. He does not regard his fancies as a permanent substitute for reality; on the contrary, he ardently hopes to translate them into fact when the time comes.

It is a dangerous error to confound truth with matter-of-fact. Our life is governed not only by facts, but by hopes; the kind of truthfulness which sees nothing but facts is a prison for the human spirit. Dreams are only to be condemned when they are a lazy substitute for an effort to change reality; when they are an incentive, they are fulfilling a vital purpose in the incarnation of human ideals. To kill fancy in childhood is to make a slave to what exists, a creature tethered to earth and therefore unable to create heaven.

This is all very well, you may say, but what has it to do with giants eating young children, or Bluebeard cutting off his wives' heads? Are these things to exist in your heaven? Must not imagination be purified and ennobled before it can serve any good purpose? How can you, a pacifist, allow your innocent boy to revel in the thought of destroying human life? How can you justify a pleasure derived from instincts of savagery which the human race must outgrow? All this I imagine the reader has been feeling. The matter is important, and I will try to state why I hold to a different point of view.

Education consists in the cultivation of instincts, not in their suppression. Human instincts are very vague, and can be satisfied in a great variety of ways. Most of them require, for their gratification, some kind of skill. Cricket and baseball satisfy the same instinct, but a boy will play whichever he has learnt. Thus the secret of instruction, in so far as it bears upon character, is to give a man such kinds of skill as shall lead to his employing his instincts usefully. The instinct of power, which in the child is crudely satisfied by identification with Bluebeard, can find in later life a refined satisfaction by scientific discovery, or artistic creation, or the creation and education of splendid children, or any one of a thousand useful activities.

BR OE 71

'I wonder what the children might think if they only knew. They too ask for bread and how often we give them stones. These unwilling children, are they active?'

'Active! They are as active as cats—if I'd let them be, but not about grammar or decimal points. A few of them like these subjects, but most of them have to be driven. Am I wrong? Oughtn't the children to learn how to use the decimal point? Or don't you people believe in having children learn? Has the verb *to learn* gone out of fashion?'

'Most certainly children should learn. If I have any complaint against the old-régime method, it is that children under it do not learn.'

'Then why talk so much about growing? I should say that growing and learning are two quite different things. Trees grow, but people learn. I don't quite understand you.'

Two senses of growing

'Let's see how matters stand. You say trees grow. Very good, and in much the same way do children's bodies grow and also their "intelligence," the thing the psychologists are now talking so much about.'

'And is this intelligence the thing that they say is full-grown at about fourteen or sixteen years?'

'Yes.'

'Do you believe it?'

'I think in the main they are right.'

'But you were talking of another kind of growing.'

'Yes, I was thinking primarily of such growing as means more thoughts, more meanings, finer and finer distinctions, better ways of behaving, higher degrees of skill, broader interests, wider and better organizations—all the things that go along with a growing interest span.'

'Then growing has two meanings?'

'I think we may say so.'

'Does the interest span grow because these added things come, or do they come because the interest span grows?'

'Until a child is fourteen or sixteen possibly both happen. After that time it is mainly (if not entirely) the coming of these new things in their various connections that makes the interest span lengthen out.'

'And it is this second kind of growing that mainly concerns us?'

'Yes, in it learning and growing mean about the same thing.'

Learning and growing

'Is your last statement quite correct? Do you think cramming brings growth of the kind you wish? Yet cramming is learning, at any rate as the psychologists define learning. What say you?'

'I know what you mean and I quite agree with you. I think there are degrees of learning.'

'And so does the psychologist, but you don't mean quite what he means by *learning*, do you?'

Two meanings of the verb 'to learn'
Will and can both needed

'I think we are concerned with different problems and so tend to use words a little differently. The psychologist is immediately concerned with laboratory conditions. For him, accordingly, learning largely means acquiring the ability to give back, on demand, the skill to do anything when a signal is given. For the laboratory, this is generally sufficient. But I am concerned with life, with remaking life, in the young typically but also in grown-ups. I wish not merely the ability to respond but also the disposition to respond. For my purposes a thing has not been sufficiently learned unless it WILL be used when the right time comes. CAN is not sufficient.'

WHK FM 188–190

Granting that childhood is playhood, what do we do about it? We ignore the fact; we forget all about it, because play, to us, is waste of time. Hence we erect a large city school with many rooms and expensive apparatus for teaching, but all we offer to the play instinct is a small concrete space with not a single fitting or object that suggests play of any kind. I am not taking into account playing fields and organized games, for I am thinking of play in terms of phantasy and not in terms of football or hockey. Organized games involve skill, competition, team work, but child play usually requires no skill, little competition and hardly any team work. True, small children will play gangster games with shooting or sword play, very often inspired by a visit to the cinema, yet long before the film era children played gang games—tig, touch, etc. Stories and films will give a direction to some kind of play, but the fundamentals are in the heart of all children of all races. What final effect on play the dangerous, sadistic American comics will have, I tremble to contemplate.

Summerhill might be defined as a school in which play is of the greatest importance. Some children play all day, especially when the sun is shining. Their play is generally noisy.

ASN FC 70–1

What is a child? A child is a being that is largely unconscious. Its life is in great measure spent in phantasy and its play is an expression of this life. Childhood is playhood. The child is naturally active and noisy and unaware (as the state of the furniture in my school testifies). It is primarily concerned with doing, not thinking —phantasy thinking, yes: reality thinking, no. That comes later.

Now in the classroom the phantasy side of the child has no outlook except the dangerous one of day-dreaming instead of attending to the lesson. The active side is inhibited by the necessity of sitting still, under an ignorant teacher in sitting with arms folded. The noisy side is completely suppressed until playtime. The creative side in a desk school has the minimum of opportunity for expression.

ASN PT 57

Some of you may be doubtful about the importance of emotion. Believe me, and I speak from a long experience, if you educate the emotions the intellect will look after itself. When a boy loses his guilty conscience about masturbation he always learns his lessons more easily and willingly. I use this illustration because, strictly speaking, one cannot educate the emotions: the most one can do is to try to destroy the bonds that have tied up emotion and changed it into guilt and hate. All you can do is to furnish outlets for emotion, and these outlets should be material rather than human. It is better for a child to be creatively emotional in painting a picture than destructively emotional in hating his teacher, but if schools had a complete apparatus for emotional outlet on material, hating the teacher would disappear.

ASN PT 159

Basic nature of pupils

Mind is dynamic: its energy cannot be destroyed. It must go forwards, or, if it cannot, then backwards. To go forwards is to grow and advance; to go backwards is to regress to earlier pleasures, to have the purpose fixed at a point which should also have the purpose fixed at a point which should have been passed and left. Wish or purpose so fixed, in an infantile form, later becomes bad health, of faults of character, or both. Growth is a progress from the more sensuous to the less sensuous. The first and most intense of our pleasure is at the breast—the sensuous pleasure felt with the mouth and the cheeks. It is a pleasure of touch. The fist, the rattle, the toy, all at first go to the same place, the mouth. The problem is to bring in the new interests—the noise of the rattle, the direction of movement in the hand. Or put the child in his cot, where he can see the motes in the sunbeam or the leaves moving on a tree. It is a delicate task to keep his interests moving, and easy to forget that he has them or needs them. But the child who in the proper sense of the word really is unspoilt—has not been spoiled by having his instincts disallowed and his growth stopped—will always of his own nature be carrying energy onwards, farther afield and to a higher form. The boy a few years later rides up and down the path on his bicycle, as he learns to ride; but on getting skill enough, goes farther afield to a higher purpose. Just so the child always increases difficulties for himself in play, and so goes on in self-education, acting always on his impulse to increase his sense of power. This principle goes on through life. Any later faults are the result of the turning aside of this creative impulse.

HL TPT 30–1

According to the 'orthodox' psychologists there are many more or less separate instinctive forces which operate in more or less separate compartments. There are instincts, for instance, producing separate desires for food, for social companionship, for sex pleasure. But the theory advanced above is that all the instinctive desires are only forms, differentiated and specialized at particular periods, of a single force, life—the force which causes an infant to suck, and later to inquire about its origins and birth, being the same force as that which after adolescence brings desire for the life and companionship of sex. Any instinctive development which, at the proper time, the child is not both permitted and encouraged to approve, use and develop, will last on in its infantile form, and, being therefore repressed by the child, will thus pass out of conscious control; this is what so often happens in the department of sex.

Human nature is innately good; the unconscious processes are in no way immoral. Faults are not corrected by, but brought about by, suppression in childhood. If the child is allowed to express himself at different stages without restriction, he will himself eliminate the unethical, and, as altruism begins to unfold from the unconscious mind at adolescence, will develop into an ethical being.

HL TPT 130

Our whole life is built about a certain number—not a very small number—of primary instincts and impulses. Only what is in some way connected with these instincts and impulses appears to us desirable or important; there is no faculty, whether 'reason' or 'virtue' or whatever it may be called, that can take our active life and our hopes and fears outside the region controlled by these first movers of all desire. Each of them is like a queen bee, aided by a hive of workers gathering honey; but when the queen is gone the workers languish and die, and the cells remain empty of their expected sweetness. So with each primary impulse in civilized man: it is surrounded and protected by a busy swarm of attendant derivative desires, which store up in its service whatever honey the surrounding world affords. But if the queen-impulse dies, the death-dealing influence, though retarded a little by habit, spreads slowly through all the subsidiary impulses, and a whole tract of life becomes inexplicably colourless. What was formerly full of zest, and so obviously worth doing that it raised no questions, has now grown dreary and purposeless: with a sense of disillusion we inquire the meaning of life, and decide, perhaps, that all is vanity. The search for an outside meaning that can *compel* an inner response must always be disappointed: all 'meaning' must be at bottom related to our primary desires, and when they are extinct no miracle can restore to the world the value which they reflected upon it.

The purpose of education, therefore, cannot be to create any primary impulse which is lacking in the uneducated; the purpose can only be to enlarge the scope of those that human nature provides, by increasing the number and variety of attendant thoughts, and by showing where the most permanent satisfaction is to be found. Under this impulse of a Calvinistic horror of the 'natural man', this obvious truth has been too often misconceived in the training of the young; 'nature' has been falsely regarded as excluding all that is best in what is natural, and the endeavour to teach virtue has led to the production of stunted and contorted hypocrites instead of full-grown human beings. From such mistakes in education a better psychology or a kinder heart is beginning to preserve the present generation; we need, therefore, waste no more words on the theory that the purpose of education is to thwart or eradicate nature.

But although nature must supply the initial force of desire, nature is not, in the civilized man, the spasmodic, fragmentary, and yet violent set of impulses that it is in the savage. Each impulse has its constitutional ministry of thought and knowledge and reflection, through which possible conflicts of impulses are foreseen, and temporary impulses are controlled by the unifying impulse which may be called wisdom. In this way education destroys the crudity of instinct, and increases through knowledge the wealth and variety of the individual's contacts with the outside world, making him no longer an isolated fighting unit, but a citizen of the universe, embracing distant countries, remote regions of space, and vast stretches of past and future within the circle of his interests. It is this simultaneous softening in the insistence of desire and enlargement of its scope that is the chief moral end of education.

Closely connected with this moral end is the more purely intellectual aim of education, the endeavour to make us see and imagine the world in an objective manner, as far as possible as it is in itself, and not merely through the distorting medium of personal desire. The complete attainment of such an objective view is no doubt an ideal, indefinitely approachable, but not actually and fully realizable. Education, considered as a process of forming our mental habits and our outlook on the world, is to be judged successful in proportion as its outcome approximates to this ideal; in proportion, that is to say, as it gives us a true view of our place in society, of the relation of the whole human society to its non-human environment, and of the nature of the non-human world as it is in itself apart from our desires and interests. If this standard is admitted, we can return to the consideration of science, inquiring how far science contributes to such an aim, and whether it is in any respect superior to its rivals in educational practice.

BR ML 34–5

In the life process—of individuals, of groups—is centred all there is to living. Here is whatever life includes of satisfyingness, of consideration for others, of fine values or lesser ones, of adequacy at control, of realization of one's longings, of effect—good or otherwise—on the lives of others. It is essential therefore for philosophy to make the study of the life process central if it is really concerned with the living of people, if it wishes its study of basic assumptions, of values, of worthwhile aims, of means of validating, to flower in more satisfying living. In Chapter XI this problem of what makes a life good to live will be discussed at some length; here it is the biological life process which concerns us.

Bertrand Russell has said:

> Desire, activity, purpose, are essential to a tolerable life, and a millennium, though it may be a joy in prospect, would be intolerable if it were actually achieved.

In other words, the successful and happy life is active life. This statement gives us a clear clue to the nature of the human organism. Any organism—human or lower—abhors inactivity; its pattern is behaving, activity, striving for something that it prefers or desires. In the human organism purposing is its characteristic.

The inclusive word *behavior* brings us directly into the life process as biology sees it. By *behaving* we mean the *responding* of an *organism* to a *confronting situation.* This responding involves an inner *stirring* which in the case of man includes not simply *intellect,* as the older outlook would have it, but the person's whole being, his *whole organism* (to repeat the biologic term); he *feels*, he *thinks*, he makes pertinent *bodily movements*. More precisely, the stirrings brings forth or wakes up a *want*; and this want leads to the setting up of *an aim or goal*; and following this the individual puts forth *efforts* to attain this aim and goal so as, we say, to *control the situation* to his chosen end. But there is more to the life process than efforts and control. Along with it all goes *interest*, interest in what one is doing and interest in what it leads to. There is, in fact, positive *enjoyment* in making efforts, provided they promise approved success. And the satisfaction which crowns success is still not all; we enjoy this success the more if there seems more ahead beckoning us on still further; as Wordsworth said,

> Effort, and expectation, and desire,
> And something evermore about to be.—*Prelude*, bk. vi, l. 607.

The life process thus includes both effort and interest: effort to attain goals, interest in the effort itself as truly as in the goals, and further interest in what this leads to.

From what has just been said we can conclude that the unit element for the study of the life process is not simply the organism—still less merely the intellect, as the older emphasis seemed to say. Nor is this unit the environment, nor even the organism and the environment, each viewed as simply a distinct entity. The true unit of study is the organism-in-active-interaction-with-the-environment. While the interacting is in process, both organism and environment are each also in process of becoming somewhat different. This word *process* we shall many times meet hereafter.

WHK PE 13–14

Sex

A certain amount of possessive happiness is necessary to the maintaining of life. Nature, left to herself, divides the two spheres of happiness very cunningly, but with our distorted ideas of education we over-develop one or the other, usually the possessive. The result of the child's finding its own substitute pleasure at the time of weaning is that it acts in a way repugnant to mother, as by rubbing or by thumb-sucking; the mother associates the action with sin, or fears that it will lead to some sin, and probably smacks the child's hands and perhaps fastens them down in some way, so that the practice is checked; at the same time she introduces the idea of sin and of God, which is thus connected in the child's mind with sex. This has a far-reaching result in later life, causing various degrees of inhibition, up to impotence.

HL TPT 125

Opponents of co-education are those who fear that if you have boys and girls educated together they will sleep together. They do not say that this is behind their doubts and fears: they rationalize. ... Girls have a slower tempo in learning ... it makes boys effeminate and girls masculine ... and so on. But deep down is the moral fear, which is a jealous fear. The old want the young to be moral because the old want to keep the best things in life for themselves. That is the only excuse for morality. All other excuses are evasions. Sex is the greatest pleasure in the world, and it is repressed because it is the greatest pleasure in the world.

So that every now and again an adult comes to the school and says: 'But don't they all sleep with each other?' and when I answer that they don't, he or she cries: 'But why not? At their age I would have had a hell of a good time.'

It is necessary to discuss sex as it appears at various ages. Freud has made us all familiar with the idea that sex is there from the beginning of life, that the baby has a sexual pleasure in sucking, and that gradually the erotic zone of the mouth gives place to that of the genitals. Thus masturbation in a child is a natural discovery, not a very important discovery at first, because the genitals are not so pleasurable as the mouth or even the skin. It is the parental verbot[1] that makes masturbation so great a complex, and the sterner the verbot the deeper the sense of guilt and the greater the compulsion to indulge.

The well-brought-up infant should come to school with no guilty feeling about masturbation at all. There are few, if any, of our Cottage children who have any special interest in masturbation, because no verbot has made the interest a guilty, hidden one. Sex to them has not the attraction of something mysterious: from their earliest time with us (if they have not been told at home) they know the facts of birth, not only where babies come from but how they are made. At that early age such information is received without emotion, partly because it is given without emotion. So it comes that at the age of fifteen or seventeen such children can discuss sex without any feeling of wrong or pornography.

It is the removal of the guilt complex about masturbation that makes Summerhill what a doubter would call 'safe.' It is this freedom from guilt that has given us a record of sixteen years without any signs of homosexuality. Some years ago a Public School boy tried to introduce sodomy, but he had no success, and was incidentally surprised and alarmed when he discovered that the whole school knew about his efforts. This absence of homosexuality is of the greatest importance. It suggests that homosexuality is masturbation on promotion ... you masturbate with the other bloke and he shares the guilt with you and thus lightens your burden. When masturbation is not considered a sin the necessity to share guilt does not arise. The root basis of the whole sex question is masturbation. When that is free the child naturally goes on to heterosexuality at the proper time. Many unhappy marriages are due to the fact that both parties are suffering from an unconscious hate of sexuality arising from buried self-hate due to masturbation verbots. The question of masturbation is *the* super-eminent one in education. Subjects, discipline, order, games ... all are vain and

[1] prohibition

futile if the masturbation question remains unsolved. Freedom in masturbation means good, happy, eager children who are not much interested in masturbation. Masturbation verbot means miserable, unhappy children often prone to colds and epidemics, hating themselves and consequently hating others. I say that the happiness and cleverness of Summerhill children is due to the removal of the bogie of fear and self-hate that masturbation verbots give.

I have said that there is no homosexuality in Summerhill. That is true, but there is in Summerhill, as in any other place where there are children, an unconscious homosexuality during a certain stage of development. Children up to puberty are largely homosexual though unconsciously homosexual. It is passive, negative. Our boys of nine and ten have no use for girls at all. They despise them. Their unconscious homosexuality makes them go in gangs, but gangs that are not interested in sex: their interest is making folks 'stick 'em up!' So girls of that age go in girls' gangs: their interest is still in their own sex. Boys and girls are not much interested in each other until they are about fifteen or sixteen.

I am often asked if I have any fears that things may happen between the older pupils. I have no fears, because I know that I am not dealing with children who have a repressed and therefore unnatural interest in sex. Some years ago we had two pupils arrive at the same time, a boy of seventeen from a Public School and a girl of sixteen from a girls' school. They fell in love with each other. They were always together. I met them late one night, and I stopped.

'I don't know what you two are doing,' I said, 'and morally I don't care, for it isn't a moral question at all. But economically I do care. If you, Kate, had a kid my school would be ruined.'

I went on to expand the theme.

'You see,' I said, 'you have just come to Summerhill. To you it means freedom to do what you like. You have, quite naturally, no feeling for the school, and if you had been here from the age of seven I'd never have had to mention it, for you would have had so strong an attachment to the school that you would think of it.'

I never spoke to them again on the subject. It was the only possible way of dealing with the problem, for sex is not a moral problem at all.

ASN TDS 75–8

One persistent criticism of Summerhill is that the children swear. It is true that they swear . . . if saying Old English words is swearing. It is true that any new pupil will swear more than necessary, and at our meetings a girl of thirteen who came from a convent was always being charged with shouting out the word 'bugger' when she went bathing. It was impressed upon her that she only did it when bathing, and that therefore she was swanking. As one boy put it: 'You are just a silly little twirp. You want to swank in front of outside people and show that Summerhill is a free school, and you just do the opposite; you make people look down on the school.'

In a P.L.[1] I explained to her that she was really trying to do the school harm because she hated it.

'But I don't hate Summerhill,' she cried. 'It's a topping place.'

'Yes,' I said, 'it is, as you say, a topping place, but you aren't in it. You are still living in your convent, and you have brought all the hate of the convent and the nuns with you. You identify Summerhill with the hated convent, and it isn't really Summerhill you are trying to damage; it is the convent.'

But she went on shouting out her buggers until Summerhill became a real place to her and not a symbol. It is the floating population that makes swearing a social difficult in Summerhill. Not that the old pupils are saintly in mouth, but the old-timers swear at the right time, so to speak. They use conscious control.

Children accept swearing as a natural language. Adults condemn it because their obscenity is greater than that of children. Only an obscene person will condemn obscenity. Parents must ask themselves the question:—Shall I allow my children to swear openly, or shall I leave them to be obscene in dark dirty corners like the boys in Huxley's novel? There is no half-way house. The hush hush way leads to the adulthood of tiresome commercial traveller stories and music-hall innuendoes, that is an obscene repressive state. The open way leads to a clear clean interest in all life. At a venture I say that our old boys and girls have the cleanest minds in England.

ASN TDS 82–4

Mothers too often do not play enough with their babies. They seem to think that baby in a pram with a soft teddy bear solves things

[1] [P.L. = Private Lesson : Ed.]

for an hour or two. Babies want to be tickled and hugged and larked with. One should ignore those life-shy psychologists who tell you never to have the baby in bed with you, never to tickle it, the idea being that any bodily contact might raise sexual emotions in the baby, thus giving it a fixed mother or father complex. There might be a danger but only if the parent were so neurotic as to find self-centred pleasure for herself in so doing, but I am writing for more or less normal people, not parents who are still infants themselves.

When baby gets the length of including his or her genitals in the play scheme, the parents meet the great test in their job. It may be that when a baby's life is full, the genital toys will come later as interests; so far I have not enough evidence to know. All I know is that, late or early, genital play must be accepted as good and normal and healthy, and any attempts to suppress it will be dangerous, and I include the underhand, dishonest attempt at drawing the child's attention to something else. A self-regulated girl was sent to a nice nursery school daily. She seemed unhappy. Her genital play she had christened 'snuggling in,' and when her mother asked her why she did not like school she said: 'When I try to snuggle in they don't tell me not to, but they say: Look at this or Come and do this, so I can't ever snuggle in there.'

This infantile masturbation (genital play is a better term) is a most complicated problem because nearly all parents were conditioned in an anti-sex way in their cradles, and cannot overcome a sense of shame and sin and disgust deep down in their own personalities. It is possible to have a strong intellectual opinion that genital play is good and healthy, and at the same time, by tone of voice or by look of the eyes, convey to the child that emotionally you have not accepted the child's right to its own genital satisfaction. A parent may seem to approve wholly when baby touches its genitals, but when stiff-stomached Aunt Mary comes to call, the parent may have anxiety lest baby performs in front of the life-disapprover. It is easy to say to such a parent: 'Aunt Mary represents the anti-sex element in your repressed self,' but saying this does not help parents or child, and we do not know enough to say definitely what is due to repression and what is not. A familiar question asked by critics of child freedom is: 'Why don't you let a small child see sexual intercourse?' The answer, that it would give the baby a trauma, a severe nervous shock, is shown to be false among the Trobriands where, according to Malinovski, children see, not only parental sexual intercourse, but birth and death as matters of course. I do not think that seeing sexual intercourse would have any bad emotional effect on a self-regulated child. The only honest answer to the question is to say that love isn't a public matter anyway, not in our civilization.

ASN FC 54–5

But at this point I shall be met by an argument which must be faced at the outset. What if a boy's curiosity is morbid or perverted? What if he is interested in obscenity, or in accounts of tortures? What if he is only interested in prying into other people's doings? Are such forms of curiosity to be encouraged? In answering this question we must make a distinction. Most emphatically, we are not to behave so that the boy's curiosity shall continue to be limited to these directions. But it does not follow that we are to make him feel wicked for wishing to know about such things, or that we are to struggle to keep knowledge of them away from him. Almost always, the whole attraction of such knowledge consists of the fact that it is forbidden; in a certain number of cases it is connected with some pathological mental condition which needs mental treatment. But in no case is prohibition and moral horror the right treatment. As the commonest and most important case, let us take an interest in obscenity. I do not believe that such a thing could exist in a boy or girl to whom sex knowledge was just like any other knowledge. A boy who obtains possession of indecent pictures is proud of his skill in having done so, and of knowing what his less enterprising companions have failed to find out. If he had been told openly and decently all about sex, he would feel no interest in such pictures. If, nevertheless, a boy were found to have such an interest, I should have him treated by a doctor skilled in these matters. The treatment should begin by encouraging him to utter freely even his most shocking thoughts, and should continue with a flood of further information, growing gradually more technical and scientific, until the whole matter bored him to extinction. When he felt that there was nothing more to know, and that what he did know was uninteresting, he would be cured. The important point is that the knowledge in itself is not bad, but only the habit of brooding on one particular topic. An obsession is not cured, at first, by violent efforts to distract attention, but rather by a plethora of the subject. Through this the interest can be made scientific instead of morbid; and when that has been achieved, it takes its legitimate place among other interests, and ceases to be an obsession. This, I am convinced, is the right way to deal with a narrow and morbid curiosity. Prohibition and moral horror can only make it worse.

BR OE 132

Interest

An adverse view of interest

'What is interest?'

'I'll tell you what interest is and you'll see that I for one don't believe in it. Interest is the best known device for spoiling children. To go around hunting for easy, interesting things for children to do, to be forever trying to amuse them, to be forever asking what they'd like to do, and whether it pleases them to do this rather than that—this is what interest means and, I repeat it, it is the best way yet devised for spoiling children. I haven't agreed with all that has been said here from time to time, but I have been thankful that so far no one has advocated this wishy-washy, namby-pamby "doctrine of interest." I think it is the worst educational doctrine I know.'

'If interest is all that and just that, it *is* pretty bad; and I shouldn't blame you for objecting to it. But is that the doctrine of interest?'

'I thought it was admitted that a child, anybody in fact, learns better when he is interested; and I have read that fatigue, mental fatigue I mean, or at least what commonly passes for mental fatigue, is largely boredom, lack of interest. Are not these things scientifically proved? If so, how can the doctrine of interest be so bad as we have just been told?'

'Do you deny that children can be spoiled? Have you never seen a spoiled child? And can you think of a better way to spoil a child than always to be trying to amuse him and encouraging him to do only what interests him? I am in earnest about this thing. I believe that the whole question of vigorous moral character is at stake, and therefore I am dead against the whole doctrine of interest. It's vicious.'

'We don't seem to be talking about the same thing exactly. Can't we get together as to what we mean?'

'Isn't the fact that the term is misunderstood one reason why we don't hear so much about interest as formerly. I heard a lecturer say he seldom used the word "interest" unless he had ample time to explain what he meant, because so many people misunderstood.'

Two notions of interest

'Suppose for the sake of getting together we agree—at least tentatively—that there are two uses of the word, a good use or meaning of interest and a bad use and meaning of interest. Perhaps later we can get the two meanings closer together. Can't we bring in our psychology? For surely if interest has any meaning we can state it psychologically. Let's take clear cases at first. What are some good instances of interest and what do they mean psychologically?'

'Washington was deeply interested in establishing the new government. How will that do?'

'That's a good instance. Now let's have another.'

'Mary is deeply interested in making a doll's dress.'

'Again, good. Now another."

'A man of many interests is more likely to be companionable than one of few interests.'

'This last brings up a distinction. Do you notice it has the noun "interests," "many interests," while the others are both verbal in form, "was interested," "is interested." More precisely the first two are instances of interest now active, now in operation. In the last case the man *has* "many interests," but we do not necessarily think of any of them as being just now active. Just as tennis is one of my interests, but I am not playing it at present nor is my interest in tennis now aroused or active. Does this bring to mind any psychology?'

'Isn't the formula S → R?[1] We have many such bonds and carry them about with us, but they are active only as stimulated.'

Psychologically, interest is mind-set

'So far so good, but I was thinking of mind-set, which is of course based on S → R. To have tennis as an abiding interest means to have built up already in the past within one an aggregate of tennis-regarding and tennis-acting S → R bonds such that when this aggregate is properly stimulated we have and feel right then and there a mind-set on tennis, and when this mind-set is so aroused, the person is at that time actively interested in tennis.'

'If I understand you then, interest is psychologically the same

[1] [Stimulus - Response : Ed.]

as mind-set. The abiding but now unaroused interest means the possession of an appropriate aggregate of S → R bonds. When this aggregate is stirred so that the mind is now set on doing something about this thing, the interest is active.'

'Exactly so. Interest to me is simply another way of naming and describing the psychology of mind-set and readiness.'

'To you, then, the doctrine of interest in education is nothing but the doctrine of mind-set and learning. Am I right?'

'Yes, practically that.'

'Where does readiness come in?'

'When one is interested, actively interested at the present time, as the little girl is in making a doll's dress, is there any readiness?'

'Surely, she is ready "all over," as we said once before when we were discussing mind-set and readiness. But this only confirms the idea that interest and mind-set are the same thing.'

'Is this why interest is a favorable condition for learning?'

'Exactly so.'

'And interests, are they good or may they be bad?'

'Of course, they may be bad, but that is not quite the question. It is the "doctrine of interest" we are asking about. What is the *doctrine* of interest? I understand a doctrine of interest to be some position or opinion as to how interest should be used. Now what is *the* doctrine of interest?'

'It seems to me that we find advocated two doctrines of interest. They overlap perhaps, but one is carelessly conceived and the other carefully conceived. One is clearly indefensible. The other stands on quite a different basis.'

'How do you state the two?'

A wrong kind of interest

'The indefensible position is the one we heard about at the outset today. It says that since interest is the condition favorable for learning, one must, therefore, strive to interest children; amuse them; cajole them; do anything so long as they are interested. This doctrine is bad. It easily leads to, and could hardly fail to lead to spoiling, to forming all sorts of bad habits.'

'But are you not forced logically to this position, I mean to this doctrine of interest, if you start out by saying that a state of interest is desirable? If it is desirable, why not get it, and get it any way you can?'

Interest as whole-hearted endeavor

'In order to answer, let's get the other doctrine of interest before us. Interest is the name this second position gives to that state of affairs in which one is intent on something, in which his mind is so set on some activity that he is striving to go ahead with the activity. It may be a child who is intent on making a doll's dress; it may be a poet intent on expressing adequately his deepest insight into life. Each is interested. This kind of interest inspires whole-hearted endeavor. Each one finds his whole being unitedly and absorbedly at work upon the object of interest. The essence of this interest is that the self is active and unified as it works. This doctrine of interest says that interest, so understood, is the guarantee of attention and effort; and that such attentive and interested effort best utilizes the laws of learning, particularly of set, readiness, and effect. So stated, the doctrine of interest is nothing but the doctrine of mind-set and learning as we have previously discussed it.'

'You don't mean to deny that there are degrees of interest?'

'Most assuredly not. There are infinitely many degrees, reaching from those things that we do only under the direst compulsion up to those into which we put our whole souls.'

'Then I don't understand your doctrine of interest. Which kind of interest are you talking about?'

'My doctrine of interest, as a psychological doctrine, is that learning conditions are met in the degree that wholehearted interest (short of painful solicitude) is present.'

'Why say "short of painful solicitude"?'

'Because we are discussing learning conditions, and I know that anxiety or fear may be so great as to interfere with learning. So I wish whole-heartedness of interest short of such fear or anxiety.'

'You say that this doctrine of interest is a psychological matter. You seem to mean that there is something else. Is there some other doctrine of interest?'

When interests are good

'There is more yet—an ethical or social aspect to the question. Suppose a bad interest, I mean a socially bad one. If the child were whole-hearted about it, he might, psychologically, learn just as well as if it were a good interest. We need then some criterion to tell a good interest from a bad one. That is what I had in mind.'

'Can you give us such a criterion?'

'So far as I can see, we best judge by the kind of growth that comes from the interest.'

. . . we should seek for our children challenging interests—not the easy, merely amusing ones—but interests that grip and stir, yes, and those that involve difficulties also, so that our children may among other things have practice in striving in the face of difficulties. The difficulties must, of course, be adjusted to their strength. It is overcoming that on the whole educates. If our children are to grow in persistence, success is as a rule necessary.'

Interest and discipline

'Do you seriously mean that our children will get sufficient discipline, I mean the right kind of discipline, from working at matters that interest them? Have you sufficiently considered the proportion of uninteresting work in the world?'

'If you will understand that the matters of interest shall involve difficulties, then I answer "Yes." That is what I mean, and I mean it very seriously. You wouldn't accuse Professor Thorndike of "soft pedagogy," would you? Here is something of his that I read the other day:

> "The discipline from enduring the disagreeable seems to be far outweighed by the discipline from working with an interested will along lines that fit one's abilities." '

Making things interesting

'You make out a pretty good case, I must admit. But there is one question yet: How can we make things interesting? I mean school subjects, really necessary things like the multiplication tables and spelling. They are not in themselves interesting. What shall we do?'

'The question is as good as the answer is difficult. There are with an aroused mind-set, either as end or aim of the mind-set and readiness be accepted, we cannot really *make* things interesting. Anything is interesting according to the degree that it belongs with an aroused mind-set, either as end or aim of the mind-set or as means felt to be necessary to attaining that end. But for such interest to take place, the aggregate of S → R bonds must already be there to be aroused. All we can do is to stimulate what is there.'

'Well, you can say that if you wish. But you know as well as I that there is a great difference, say, in lecturers. One man will make a subject interesting (I am obliged to use these very words);

and another, try as he will, cannot interest his hearers. The audience may be the same and the topic may be the same. The difference is in what the lecturers do. One makes the subject interesting and the other doesn't. How then can you say that we cannot *make* a thing interesting? It can be done. I have seen it done and so have you. It is done or not done every day. I am not just talking words; I am talking facts, and you know it.'

'Yes, you are talking facts, but I stick also to what I said. The only way to "make" a thing interesting is to give it a chance to arouse some interest already present in the mind or, better, in the nervous system. Go back to our psychology. There must be present in the nervous system the proper aggregate of $S \rightarrow R$ bonds before the stimulus can take effect, i.e., before there can be stimulation to action. The resulting action is the responding of the R. The interest, as a matter of $S \rightarrow R$ structure, must be present in the nervous system before it can be aroused to activity. Take your two lecturers. They address the same auditors. One interests, as you say. The other doesn't. The difference is that the successful lecturer so presents the subject as to stir what was all the time there to be stirred. The unsuccessful lecturer does not know how to disclose the attractions of the subject or to organize these so as to arouse those responses of thought and emotion and action-tendencies which, when aroused and active, we call interest. It is after all a *disclosing* of attractions, a presenting of stimuli. And this is essentially what we mean when we speak of *making* a thing interesting.'

'Does this have any bearing on curriculum construction?'

Interest and curriculum

'It has a very great bearing. The main business of curriculum making is two-fold—first, to know what interests, native or acquired, lie available in the child nature; second, to know how these may be stimulated, guided and directed so as to bring growing. One main part of curriculum making is to know and stir interests that otherwise might lie dormant. We must think of all stirring to action as an appeal to what is present as $S \rightarrow R$ in the mind and character of the person. Most people get into trouble by choosing first what children should learn, then hunting about for the best way to teach it. If this subject-matter so chosen in advance does not correspond to the child's present active powers, naturally there is trouble. In the older days people said of such cases that human nature is naturally depraved and that we need not expect desirable subject-matter to correspond to child nature. They accordingly reduced their subject-matter to what could be assigned for learning (mostly memorizing) under penalty. In that day, school was worse than a dull place. Switches were much in evidence. When we examine the subject-matter of that day, we don't wonder that children had to be whipped. Later there came kinder methods, rivalry and prizes, and also some modifications of subject-matter. Much later a doctrine of interest was preached, but it was still likely to be a doctrine of *making* things interesting. That is, the old subject-matter was assumed, and interest was used as a teaching device. That people learn better when interested was seen to be true. "Therefore," it was said, "interest the children in what they are to learn." In this way "sugar-coating" was offered as a substitute for punishment, and people divided into two camps, one favoring the "soft pedagogy" of sugar-coating ("interest", they called it) and the other the hard pedagogy of coercion ("effort," they called it).'

'Isn't this what Professor Dewey refers to in his "lawsuit" between "interest" and "effort"?'

'Yes, and then he goes on to say that both are wrong, and in place of both offers the doctrine that interest and effort are alike the natural accompaniments of healthy activity meeting normal difficulties. We use the term "interest" when we think of the emotional warming up to the end in view. We use the term "effort" when a challenging difficulty has been met, and the self still persists in going forward in spite of the naturally discouraging effect of the hindrance. Interest and effort are thus but two aspects of the same on-going activity.'

'This all sounds very well, but I still don't see how we can avoid spoiling children. Why don't you tell us how to manage?'

'The answer has in good part been given. We get our best discipline "from working with an interested will along lines that fit one's abilities." Education is concerned to get going in children such activities as (*a*) evoke work with an interested will, (*b*) lie along lines that fit their abilities. To these I should wish to add a third, or rather make explicit what was probably implied, (*c*) that the work, while beginning and remaining within the child's interest, should still always reach out beyond the past achievement of the child. If these three conditions are met, interest and effort will take care of themselves, and growth will ensue.'

'But I still don't see how you avoid spoiling. How are you going to get "work with an interested will"? I say you can't start out on that basis without spoiling the child. If you keep trying to interest the child—to amuse him—if you continually ask him whether he chooses to do this or prefers to do that, if you keep forever deferring to his wishes, you are bound to spoil him. Your start is wrong, and the result is bound to be wrong.'

Children always active

'If what you say were what I propose to do, I should agree with you. But you fundamentally misrepresent my position, and at the same time ignore the essential nature of childhood. Children when awake are inevitably and incessantly active. They will set up ends. They will strive to attain these ends. To do merely nothing is impossible with them. To keep children from activity, to make them do nothing, is a foregone failure, and is, moreover, irritating to them in the degree that it succeeds. We start then not with a child waiting to be amused, but with one incessantly active. Only a child already spoiled or already starved into inaction waits to be amused. It is opportunity they crave, opportunity to receive stimulation and opportunity then to respond. It is our business to supply or perhaps better *allow* both, and then give the more promising of the child's active stirrings a chance to go ahead.'

Whole-hearted interest makes for strong moral character

'You claim then that your doctrine of whole-hearted, interested endeavor makes rather for than against strong moral character?'

'I most assuredly do. The argument is on our side. Strong moral characters practice inhibitions, but these are best acquired in connection with strong positive interests. Mere inhibitions never built a strong character. Strong character is mainly positive.'

'If you stress child decisions so much, why have a teacher? Have you left any place for a teacher?'

Place of the teacher

Place of morale

'I most certainly do have a place for the teacher, a definite and an abiding place. The teacher guides first in the making of choices and second in the pursuit of the aim. Of course if need be the teacher will command or refuse as occasion demands. But stimulation and guidance are the teacher's more constructive functions. I like to think too of the teacher as a builder of morale. Each school can have its morale, and, well built, it is a most precious heritage.

So also is there a class morale and there is an individual pupil morale. Morale implies both habit of outward conduct and inner attitude towards this. I should like many habits and attitudes built that put the common good above mere individual interest, and others that demand persistence as long as it is wise to persist.'

How morale is built

'How are these things to be built?'

'There are no ways but the old ways: "Practice with satisfaction," "Let annoyance attend the wrong." The children must practice, outwardly and inwardly, putting the common good above mere selfish interest. If they fail, then regret for such failure should attend. But note you: It is practically impossible to get the right practice and the right satisfaction or annoyance except through interest.'

'Yes, and there's the rub. You can't build interest without practice and you can't get practice unless you already have the interest. So you are caught; either you already have what you want or you can't get it. That's where I say your interest doctrine breaks down. You have to call in the parent or teacher to issue a command, else the children never take a higher step.'

'Not so fast. Let's see if we are so hopeless as you say. Is it not true that interest in an end will to some degree extend itself to means?'

'I don't quite understand. Illustrate it.'

'Imagine a mother with a child dangerously ill. Is she interested in railway time-tables or other plans for a trip?'

How interest extends itself

'Not at all, if she is the right kind of mother. You couldn't persuade her to leave home.'

'Oh, I am not so sure. Suppose the doctor recommends a change of climate for the child. If so, she will at once be interested in where to go and how to get there. Her interest in her baby will make her interested in the trip necessary to his recovery.'

'Is the mother of a well baby interested in any other things for the baby's sake—things she used not to be interested in?'

'Indeed she is. I have seen many a young woman made over. Before the baby came her interests were only dancing or cards or the theater; now you can hardly get her to leave home, and she studies food values and the sterilization of bottles, not to mention infants' clothes, go-carts, or rattles. Yes, anything that affects the baby is interesting to her.'

'Then interest in end does extend itself to means?'

'Indeed, yes.'

'And does she practice new things?'

'Yes. I knew a young mother who could never bear to sew for herself or anyone else; but when her baby came, it was different. She sewed for him as if she were born for the work.'

'And did she become interested in sewing?'

'This particular woman did. She found out she had more of a gift than she had thought. As her husband, being merely a college instructor, had a small salary, she made most of her own clothes thereafter and was proud of her success. In fact she became a kind of authority on the subject in her young circle.'

'Do you mean that education is exactly a succession of interest, new practice, new interest, still further practice, still new interest, and so on forever?'

Education a succession of interest, practice, and interest

'That's just what I mean—that, with wise teacher guidance.'

'And you wish in developing such a succession to stay always within the realm of interest?'

'That's what I wish, and I believe that in the degree I can stay always within the realm of interest, in that same degree do I secure conditions favorable for learning.'

'Doesn't the fact of indirect interest help us here?'

'You mean that it increases the range of interest? Yes, that is a very good idea. You are quite right.'

'I don't understand. What do you mean by indirect interest? Is there a direct interest, and if so what is the difference?'

Indirect vs. *direct interest*

'By direct interest we mean the condition that exists when a person is really interested in a thing without asking or thinking why he is interested. The mother is interested in her baby's health in this way. She just is, that's all there is to it. In like manner is a little girl interested in playing with her doll. There is no why about it. But when the physician recommended a change of climate, then the mother became interested in mountain resorts and railroad schedules, *because* these things had to do with her baby's welfare. Her direct interest in the baby so extended itself as to give an indirect interest in these other things. Things uninteresting in themselves become interesting (indirect interest) because of their bearings on things that are interesting in themselves (direct interest).'

'Then you mean that around each direct interest there is a wide region of possible indirect interest?'

'Yes, get the direct interest going strongly and it will reach out, often far out.'

'And this is the enlarged interest range?'

'Yes.'

'May not an interest that begins as an indirect interest end by becoming a direct interest? The young mother who became interested in sewing as discussed above is an example of what I mean.'

'Quite so; and, in fact, each new practice begins normally as an indirect interest.'

WHK FM 136–158

THE GROWTH OF INTERESTS, AND THE GROWTH OF POWER

The child's interest must not be allowed to centre in the mother alone, for this retards growth. Mother is the source of the first and greatest and most intense of his pleasures, but in the natural growth of interests the monopoly of this first interest has to be broken down. If this is not done, if the child is too much made a plaything or too much petted, or kept in constant memory of the breast by the use of a 'soother,' then all wish will become fixed on mother and accumulate round her, and there can be no true growth. Desire will, throughout life, be piled up at the old centre. With too much dependence on mother goes an equal degree of irritability against mother; this will later be repressed into the unconscious mind, but it will be a dominant motive of adult life. It is a constant problem with a baby how much to coddle it, how much to help it to be independent. The great principle is to make the wrong thing very easy for the child to do and the right thing difficult, as it is the fighting against difficulties which charms the child. The habit of thumb-sucking has often been rendered permanent by a tied sleeve or a glove or alum, or some other device to make the habit difficult; for as soon as it is made difficult it is made desirable.

HL TPT 31–2

He co-operates with others for a common purpose. He has the greatest interest in team games. But we still see the desire to show off, if we have earlier suppressed his self-assertiveness and so have prevented the expression of altruism normal at that age. If the child is more interested in doing 'stunts' than in helping the team to win, then something has gone wrong, and the energies, first evoked at the mother's breast and afterwards to be spread over a wider field, have not been well synthesized; so the transfer from original egoism to the group-spirit is incomplete. If, however, there is no interest still left rooted in the infantile periods—no nursing desires, for instance, still left over, no unsatisfied curiosity coming down from the age of three or four about origins and birth—then the child of eleven and onwards will have no interest at all in sex as such (except from time to time to make natural inquiries), and the localization of the hitherto diffused sex area will proceed peacefully and without trouble. What is soon to be normal sex consciousness will not be felt as consciousness of sex at all, but as the desire to co-operate with friends and companions; the boy at this age will be ready to sit and keep the score if that will help the team; in any case, the team is his unit. The boy or girl who does not take any interest in games at this time is the one who has not left the previous age, one who has not become adolescent in the psychic sense. He still wants self-assertion, not to be one of a group. And it is a difficult type of adult, too, who has not developed his early, childish tendencies even far enough to take an interest in games. The social emotion in him will not have evolved; it will lie deeply buried still, under self-assertive tendencies or fantasy.

HL TPT 106–7

When it is sought to produce a certain kind of behaviour in a child or animal, there are two different techniques which may be followed. We may, on the one hand, by means of rewards and punishments cause the child or animal to perform or abstain from certain precise acts; or we may, on the other hand, seek to produce in the child or animal such emotions as will lead, on the whole, to acts of the kind desired.

BR GSO 57

The difficulty which is felt by the advocate of modern methods is that accuracy, as hitherto taught, involves boredom, and that it is an immense gain if education can be made interesting. Here, however, we must make a distinction. Boredom merely imposed by the teacher is wholly bad; boredom voluntarily endured by the pupil in order to satisfy some ambition is valuable if not overdone. It should be part of education to fire pupils with desires not easily gratified—to know the calculus, to read Homer, to perform well on the violin, or what not. Each of these involves its own kind of accuracy. Able boys and girls will go through endless tedium and submit willingly to severe discipline in order to acquire some coveted knowledge or skill. Those who have less native ability can often be fired by similar ambitions if they are inspiringly taught. The driving force in education should be the pupil's wish to learn, not the master's authority; but it does not follow that education should be soft and easy and pleasant at every stage. This applies, in particular, to the question of accuracy. The acquisition of exact knowledge is apt to be wearisome, but it is essential to every kind of excellence, and this fact can be made obvious to a child by suitable methods. In so far as modern methods fail in this respect, they are at fault. In this matter, as in many others, reaction against the old bad forms of discipline has tended to an undue laxity, which will have to give place to a new discipline, more internal and psychological than the old external authority. Of this new discipline, accuracy will be the intellectual expression.

There are various kinds of accuracy, each of which has its own importance. To take the main kinds: There is muscular accuracy, aesthetic accuracy, accuracy as to matter of fact, and logical accuracy. Every boy or girl can appreciate the importance of muscular accuracy in many directions; it is required for the control of the body which a healthy child spends all its spare time in acquiring, and afterwards for the games upon which prestige depends. But it has other forms which have more to do with school teaching, such as well-articulated speech, good writing, and correct performance on a musical instrument. A child will think these things important or unimportant according to his environment. Aesthetic accuracy is difficult to define; it has to do with the appropriateness of a sensible stimulus for the production of emotion. One way of teaching an important form of it is to cause children to learn poetry by heart—e.g. Shakespeare, for the purpose of acting—and to make them feel, when they make mistakes, why the original is better. I believe it would be found that, where aesthetic sensibility is widespread, children are taught conventional stereotyped performances, such as dances and songs, which they enjoy, but which must be done exactly right on account of tradition.

Accuracy as to matter of fact is intolerably boring when pursued on its own account. Learning the dates of the Kings of England, or the names of the counties and their capitals, used to be one of the terrors of childhood. It is better to secure accuracy by interest and repetition. I could never remember the list of capes, but at eight years old I knew almost all the stations on the Underground. If children were shown a cinema representing a ship sailing round the coast they would soon know the capes. I don't think they are worth knowing, but if they were that would be the way to teach them. All geography ought to be taught on the cinema; so ought history at first. The initial expense would be great, but not too great for Governments. And there would be a subsequent economy in ease of teaching.

Logical accuracy is a late acquisition, and should not be forced upon young children. Getting the multiplication table right is, of course, accuracy as to matter of fact; it only becomes logical accuracy at a much later stage. Mathematics is the natural vehicle for this teaching, but it fails if allowed to appear as a set of arbitrary rules. Rules must be learnt, but at some stage the reasons for them must be made clear; if this is not done, mathematics has little educative value.

I come now to a question which has already arisen in connection with exactness, the question, namely, how far it is possible or desirable to make all instruction interesting. The old view was that a great deal of it must be dull, and that only stern authority will induce the average boy to persist. (The average girl was to remain ignorant). The modern view is that it can be made delightful through and through. I have much more sympathy with the modern view than with the old one; nevertheless, I think it is subject to some limitations, especially in higher education. I shall begin with what I think true in it.

Modern writers on infant psychology all emphasize the importance of not urging a young child to eat or sleep; these things ought to be done spontaneously by the child, not as a result of coaxing or forcing. My own experience entirely bars out this teaching. At first we did not know the newer teaching, and tried the older methods. They were very unsuccessful, whereas the modern methods succeeded perfectly. It must not be supposed, however, that the modern parent does nothing about eating and sleeping; on the contrary, everything possible is done to promote the formation of good habits. Meals come at regular times, and the child must sit through them without games, whether he eats or not. Bed comes at regular times, and the child must lie down in bed. He may have a toy animal to hug, but not one that squeaks or runs or does anything exciting. If the animal is a favourite, one may play the game that the animal is tired and the child must put it to sleep. Then leave the child alone, and sleep will usually come very quickly. But never let the child think you are anxious he should sleep or eat. That at once makes him think you are asking a favour; this gives him a sense of power which leads him to demand more and more coaxing or punishment. He should eat and sleep because he wants to, not to please you.

This psychology is obviously applicable in great measure to instruction. If you insist upon teaching a child, he will conclude that he is being asked to do something disagreeable to please you, and he will have a psychological resistance. If this exists at the start, it will perpetuate itself; at a later age, the desirability of getting through examinations may become evident, and there will be work for that purpose, but none from sheer interest in knowledge. If, on the contrary, you can first stimulate the child's desire to know, and then, as a favour, give him the knowledge he wants, the whole situation is different. Very much less external discipline is required, and attention is secured without difficulty. To succeed in this method certain conditions are necessary, which Madame Montessori successfully produces among the very young. The tasks must be attractive and not too difficult. There must, at first, be the example of other children at a slightly more advanced stage. There must be no other obvious pleasant occupation open to the child at the moment. There are a number of things the child may do, and he works by himself at whichever he prefers. Almost all children are perfectly happy in this régime, and learn to read and write without pressure before they are five years old.

How far similar methods can advantageously be applied to older children is a debatable question. As children grow older they become responsive to more remote motives, and it is no longer necessary that every detail should be interesting in itself. But I think the broad principle that the impulse to education should come from the pupil can be continued up to any age. The environment should be such as to stimulate the impulse, and to make boredom and isolation the alternative to learning. But any child that preferred this alternative on any occasion should be allowed to choose it. The principle of individual work can be extended, though a certain amount of class work seems indispensable after the early years. But if external authority is necessary to induce a boy or girl to learn, unless there is a medical cause, the probability is that the teacher is at fault, or that previous moral training has been bad. If a child has been properly trained up to the age of five or six, any good teacher ought to be able to win his interest at later stages.

If this is possible, the advantages are immense. The teacher appears as the friend of the pupil, not as his enemy. The child learns faster because he is co-operating. He learns with less fatigue, because there is not the constant strain of bringing back a reluctant and bored attention. And his sense of personal initiative is cultivated instead of being diminished. On account of these advantages it seems worth while to assume that the pupil can be led to learn by the force of his own desires, without the exercise of compulsion by the teacher. If, in a small percentage of cases, the methods were found to be a failure, these cases could be isolated and instructed by different methods. But I believe that, given methods adapted to the child's intelligence, there would be very few failures.

For reasons already given in connection with accuracy, I do not believe that a really thorough education can be made interesting through and through. However much one may wish to know a subject, some parts of it are sure to be found dull. But I believe that, given suitable guidance, a boy or girl can be made to feel the importance of learning the dull parts, and can be got through them also without compulsion. I should use the stimulus of praise and blame, applied as the result of good or bad performance of set tasks. Whether a pupil possesses the necessary skill should be made as obvious as in games or gymnastics. And the importance of the dull parts of a subject should be made clear by the teacher. If all these methods failed, the child would have to be classified as stupid, and taught separately from children of normal intelligence, though care must be taken not to let this appear as a punishment.

BR OE 135–6, 137–9

Discipline and punishment

But the modern educationist does not simply eschew discipline; he secures it by new methods. On this subject, those who have not studied the new methods are apt to have mistaken ideas. I had always understood that Madame Montessori dispensed with discipline, and I had wondered how she managed a roomful of children. On reading her own account of her methods, I found that discipline still held an important place, and that there was no attempt to dispense with it. On sending my little boy of three to spend his mornings in a Montessori school, I found that he quickly became a more disciplined human being, and that he cheerfully acquiesced in the rules of the school. But he had no feeling whatever of external compulsion: the rules were like the rules of a game, and were obeyed as a means of enjoyment. The old idea was that children could not possibly *wish* to learn, and could only be compelled to learn by terror. It has been found that this was entirely due to lack of skill in pedagogy. By dividing what has to be learnt—for instance, reading and writing—into suitable stages, every stage can be made agreeable to the average child. And when children are doing what they like, there is, of course, no reason for external discipline. A few simple rules—no child must interfere with another child, no child must have more than one sort of apparatus at a time—are easily apprehended, and felt to be reasonable, so that there is no difficulty in getting them observed. The child thus acquires self-discipline, which consists partly of good habits, partly of the realization, in concrete instance, that it is sometimes worth while to resist an impulse for the sake of some ultimate gain. Everybody has always known that it is easy to obtain this self-discipline in games, but no one had supposed that the acquisition of knowledge could be made sufficiently interesting to bring the same motives into operation. We now know that this is possible, and it will come to be done, not only in the education of infants, but at all stages. I do not pretend that it is easy. The pedagogical discoveries involved have required genius, but the teachers who are to apply them do not require genius. They require only the right sort of training, together with a degree of sympathy and patience which is by no means unusual. The fundamental idea is simple: that the right discipline consists, not in external compulsion, but in habits of mind which lead spontaneously to desirable rather than undesirable activities. What is astonishing is the great success in finding technical methods of embodying this idea in education. For this, Madame Montessori deserves the highest praise.

The change in educational methods has been very much influenced by the decay of the belief in original sin. The traditional view, now nearly extinct, was that we are all born Children of Wrath, with a nature full of wickedness; before there can be any good in us we have to become Children of Grace, a process much accelerated by frequent castigation. Most moderns can hardly believe how much this theory influenced the education of our fathers and grandfathers. Two quotations from the life of Dr Arnold by Dean Stanley will show that they are mistaken. Dean Stanley was Dr Arnold's favourite pupil, the good boy Arthur in *Tom Brown's School Days*. He was a cousin of the present writer, who was shown over Westminster Abbey by him as a boy. Dr Arnold was the great reformer of our public schools which are viewed as one of the glories of England, and are still conducted largely according to his principles. In discussing Dr Arnold, therefore, we are dealing, not with something belonging to the remote past, but with something which to this day is efficacious in moulding upper-class Englishmen. Dr Arnold diminished flogging, retaining it only for the younger boys, and confining it, so his biographer tells us, to 'moral offences, such as lying, drinking and habitual idleness'. But when a liberal journal suggested that flogging was a degrading punishment, which ought to be abolished altogether, he was amazingly indignant. He replied in print:

> I know well of what feeling this is the expression; it originates in that proud notion of personal independence which is neither reasonable nor Christian, but essentially barbarian. It visited Europe with all the curses of the age of chivalry, and is threatening us now with those of Jacobinism. . . . At an age when it is almost impossible to find a true manly sense of the degradation of guilt or faults, where is the wisdom of encouraging a fantastic sense of the degradation of personal correction? What can be more false, or more adverse to the simplicity, sobriety, and humbleness

of mind, which are the best ornament of youth, and the best promise of a noble manhood.

BR OE 22–3

The teacher's chief concern should be the psychology of the child, and all school subjects should be relegated to an inferior place. The issue is evaded by the adoption of the easiest method—that of discipline. Keep the class in order so that you can hand your stuff over the footlights. Obviously if an actor wants to put his stuff across the footlights he has to make it such that his audience will discipline themselves in order to hear it. The method of the theatre should be the only one applicable to the school: the well-grac'd actor would command interest, while the actor whose prattle was merely tedious would find himself declaiming to empty benches.

Discipline is the substitute for knowledge of children. True enough it is necessary so long as school is an institution that for the most part militates against child nature: so long as children are compelled to sit at desks and to learn what they have no wish to learn, school discipline will be found necessary.

Obedience should be dynamic: its purpose should be the wish of the one who obeys and at the same time the wish of the one who commands. I think of the orchestral conductor and the band. Obedience should be reciprocal: if the child obeys the teacher the teacher ought to obey the child. To the old-fashioned teacher this may sound nonsense, but I have had this reciprocity in my school for many years, and it has been a complete success. Our school laws are made by the community by majority vote, and I have to obey them just as dutifully as the child of five has. I can order a child out of my room when I don't want his presence, and he can order me out of his room for a similar reason. We both obey.

That this system could not be readily applied to a disciplined and desk school is evident. For one thing it requires not only a study of child nature: it requires an infinite faith in children, and perhaps of more moment, an infinite faith in one's own attitude to the child. It implies a *Weltanschauung* that relegates knowledge to its proper place, that believes that what a child knows is much less important than what a child is. In other words it makes human behaviour the chief factor in education.

Yet I wonder if teachers were trained for ten years in child psychology would they be prepared to drop their pedestal position? Many, of course, would, as many do already. Teaching is not a science: it is a special kind of art, and it may be that only the artist can teach properly. I do not mean by teaching the presentation of a lesson: I mean the art of living with children and understanding them, and being one of them. Belonging to the gang, as that great teacher Homer Lane put it. A gramophone can present a good lesson just as a soulless teacher can. But a soulless gramophonic teacher can never really get into vital contact with the child.

ASN PT 54–6

A moral situation

'Suppose at home some evening the younger children persist in making so much noise that the older children cannot study and their parents cannot read. What should we do and why?'

'That's easy. I'd tell them to stop. If they didn't I'd send them to bed. Coercion or not, I certainly would not allow any of my children to ruin everybody else's happiness, and I'd do it for their own good as well. Spoiling children does what the word says; it "spoils" them.'

'Well, that is what most people would do and for the same reasons. But let's examine the matter a little. There are several ways of sizing up this situation. We may consider the rights of the parents and the older children to reasonable quiet and the attitudes of the younger children towards these rights. So stated, we have an educational situation strongly suggested. The younger children either don't understand or don't appreciate or won't respect the rights of the others. Each of these failures is a matter within the realm of education. A diagnosis should accordingly be made to locate the exact defects, and the proper educational procedure should be followed to correct them. Am I right?'

'You may be right, but you haven't told us what to do. Would you punish the children or not?'

'Certainly not until I had made an educational diagnosis and not then unless I could see in reason that the proposed punishment promised to supply the needed educational stimulation called for in their particular cases.'

'Don't you believe wrongdoing must be punished?'

'As you ask it, no. The sole reason the parent can properly have for punishing a child is the foreseen educative effect that is to follow.'

'What about spoiling a child? Isn't it a real danger?'

Educational diagnosis and treatment

'Yes, but it is brought about by bad education. I understand a spoiled child to be one who thinks his wish furnishes sufficient grounds for getting what he wishes, and who is moreover disposed to make things uncomfortable for others till he gets it. Now both of these attitudes can come in only one way: he has tried them with such uniform success that they have been fixed in him. They can be removed only by reversing the process. He must learn by the action of satisfaction and annoyance that his wish is not sufficient, that others have rights which he must take into account, and that making himself a nuisance is not a socially satisfactory way to secure ends. It may take time and patience on the part of his elders for him to learn these things, but there is no other course available.'

'And what is the psychology of the procedure?'

'There are two possible ways of procedure: one is to attach annoyance to the children's wrong behavior, the other is to see that satisfaction attends the right. Of course both at times may be combined.'

'You refer in the first to the use of punishment?'

Punishment and its limitations

'Yes, and it is best available when the annoyance will be attached uniquely to the wrongdoing. Otherwise there is danger that wrong aversions may be built up, perhaps to the mother for interfering, or to the home as a place where unpleasant things happen, or to the older sister for complaining, or to duty as a disagreeable word that figures whenever pleasures are curtailed. It is this uncertain effect of punishment, and indeed of all coercion, that makes it so unreliable an agency for moral betterment. If the attendant annoyance happens to be misplaced, mis-education takes place.'

'The second possible procedure then is more satisfactory?'

'It promises better in every way, though it is less easy for the unthinking to apply than the "Shut-up-or-be-sent-to-bed" procedure.'

'Do you recognize any proper place for coercion other than those already mentioned?'

'We didn't say explicitly, I believe, that coercion may at times be properly used to prevent the exercise of certain undesirable practices and consequently prevent the formation of undesirable habits. But even here a positive régime of building good interests instead is, if feasible, far more desirable.'

'Are there then no other uses for coercion—none whatever?'

'Oh, yes. Coercion may properly be used as an emergency measure to prevent damage to one's self or to others or to valuable property. In themselves these are not educational measures, though we can never forget that they have educative effects, usually mixed, some bad and some good.'

'You seem then to count coercion always as an evil, but sometimes as the least of the evils confronting one.'

The conclusion

'I think it has always attendant evils. Frequently, perhaps usually, these evils outweigh its good. Sometimes the reverse is true. The constant use of coercion, however, is a sign of bad teaching somewhere.'

WHK FM 96–8

What I have said of corporal punishment applies also to any of the usual forms of penalty. Sending the child to bed, depriving him of meals, or of any part of his meal, placing him in a conspicuous place of humiliation, and all the other non-related penalties are dangerous to the relationship between child and parent.

I believe that if the child violates any natural law, of the sort that brings immediate consequences, he should not be interfered with, except in such cases as will involve danger to life, limb or health. The environment of a child over five years of age should be so arranged that he cannot perform any fatal experiments. He should not have a chance to experiment with matches and gunpowder until his education will save him from the penalties of ignorance. Fire-arms, keen-edged tools, poisons, are not yet necessary appliances in his education. He should know all the properties of fire; if he does not, instruct him. Supervise his experiments with it until he knows what to avoid. We can never prevent, except temporarily, his ultimate investigation. If he does not give evidence of caution near an open window, high up from the ground, teach him caution in any improvised gymnasium. Remove all opportunities for serious injury from his path until he learns the particular danger involved. The same principle will apply to the second type of errors, the violation of natural laws that have a remote penalty. In the third and more complicated type of errors, viz. errors in connection with property, errors in connection with persons (striking, etc.), social errors (impoliteness, disrespect, lack of consideration, selfishness), let the nature of the wrong deed be realized by the child, so far as possible, in the penalty. For example, if he drives nails in the piano, let him be aware of the grief of the owner. Do not scold or punish him, for he may, in his resentment, get a secret satisfaction in the sight of the damage. Be very careful in treating him for theft, because, not being conscious of values, and not being an owner of property, he does not know the social reasons for not stealing. If he is careless with the inkpot, treat the matter naturally, and if relationships are normal he will attempt to remove the stains, feeling a genuine regret for the error, with wholesome results in future.

Errors against persons are quite common. If he strikes a younger and helpless child, a not too ostentatious sympathy with the child struck will usually bring him to regret his act. The child who commits social errors should be treated much in the same way as the adult treats those who are uncongenial. The social consciousness of the child should be quite sufficiently developed at five, if the atmosphere of his home is normal and he is an intimate friend of the other members of the family, to enable him to appreciate the disadvantage of being uncongenial, if he is made to feel the 'cold shoulder.'

HL TPT 142–3

Unless a child is ill, let it leave its food and go hungry. My boy had been coaxed into eating by his nurse, and had grown more and more *difficile*. One day when we had him for his midday meal he refused to eat his pudding, so we sent it out. After a while he demanded it back, but it turned out that the cook had eaten it. He was flabbergasted, and never made such pretences with us again. Exactly the same method should apply to instruction. Those who do not want it should be allowed to go without, though I should see to it that they were bored if they were absent during lesson-time. If they see others learning they will presently clamour to be taught: the teacher can then appear as conferring a benefit, which is the truth of the situation. I should have in every school a large bare room to which pupils could go if they did not want to learn, but if they went there I should not allow them to come back to lessons that day. And they should be sent there as a punishment if they behaved badly in lesson-time. It seems a simple principle that a punishment should be something you wish the culprit to dislike, not something you wish him to like. Yet 'lines' are a common punishment where the professed aim is to produce a love of classical literature.

Mild punishments have their utility for dealing with mild offences, especially such as are concerned with manners. Praise and blame are an important form of rewards and punishments for young children, and also for older boys and girls if conferred by a person who inspires respect. I do not believe it possible to conduct education without praise and blame, but in regard to both a certain degree of caution is necessary. In the first place, neither should be comparative. A child should not be told that he has done better than so-and-so, or that such-and-such is never naughty: the first produces contempt, the second hatred. In the second place, blame should be given much more sparingly than praise; it should be a definite punishment, administered for some unexpected lapse from good behaviour, and it should never be continued after it has produced its effect. In the third place, praise should not be given for anything that should be a matter of course. I should give it for a new development of courage or skill, and for an act of unselfishness as regards possessions, if achieved after a moral effort. All through education any unusually good piece of work should be praised. To be praised for a difficult achievement is one of the most delightful experiences in youth, and the desire for this pleasure is quite proper as an added incentive, though it should not be the main motive. The main motive should always be an interest in the matter itself, whatever the matter may happen to be.

Grave faults of character, such as cruelty, can seldom be dealt with by means of punishment. Or rather, punishment should be a very small part of the treatment. Cruelty to animals is more or less natural to boys, and requires for its prevention an education *ad hoc.* It is a very bad plan to wait until you find your boy torturing an animal, and then proceed to torture the boy. This only makes him wish he had not been caught. You should watch for the first beginnings of what may afterwards develop into cruelty. Teach the boy respect for life; do not let him see you killing animals, even wasps or snakes. If you cannot prevent it, explain very carefully why it is done in this particular case. If he does something slightly unkind to a younger child, do the same to him at once. He will protest, and you can explain that if he does not want it done to him he must not do it to others. In this way the fact that others have feelings like his own is brought vividly to his attention.

It is obviously essential to this method that it should be begun early, and applied to minor forms of unkindness. It is only very small injuries to others that you can retort in kind upon the child. And when you can adopt this plan, do not let it seem that you are doing it as a punishment, but rather as an instruction: 'See, that is what you did to your little sister.' When the child protests, you say: 'Well, if it was unpleasant, you mustn't do it to her.' So long as the whole incident is simple and immediate the child will understand, and will learn that other people's feelings must be considered. In that case, serious cruelty will never develop.

All moral instruction must be immediate and concrete: it must arise out of a situation which has grown up naturally, and must not go beyond what ought to be done in this particular instance. The child himself will apply the moral in other similar cases. It is much easier to grasp a concrete instance and apply analogous considerations to an analogous instance than to apprehend a general rule and proceed deductively. Do not say, in a general way, 'Be brave, be kind', but urge him to some particular piece of daring, and then say, 'Bravo, you were a brave boy'; get him to let his little sister play with his mechanical engine, and when he sees her beaming with delight say, 'That's right, you were a kind boy.' The same principle applies in dealing with cruelty: look out for its faint beginnings and prevent them from developing.

BR OE 95–6

Is it possible to rear a child with self-regulation and punishment together, that is two mutually antagonistic systems? No, it cannot be done. Punishment must be done away with, and, in case this sounds like a counsel of sentimental perfection, I must make clear what I mean by punishment. If baby plays with the cat and gets scratched it is not punishment; if it plays with matches and gets burned, it is not being punished. Natural reactions do not constitute punishment, because there is no suggestion of right or wrong in them. Punishment implies the judgment of an authority, be that authority parent, teacher, police, parliament. Under self-regulation there is no authority in the home, meaning that there is no loud voice that declaims: I say it; you must obey. In actual practice there is of course something resembling authority; this might be called protection, fore-care, adult responsibility! it sometimes demands obedience but at other times gives obedience itself. Thus I can say to my daughter: 'You can't bring that mud and water into our sitting-room,' that is not more of a demand by authority than is her saying to me: 'Get out of the nursery, Daddy; I don't want you here,' a wish that I of course obey without a word.

Akin to punishment is the parental demand that a child should not bite off more than it can chew . . . literally, for often a child's eye is greedier than its stomach and it will demand a plateful that it cannot eat. To force the child to finish what is on its plate is wrong. Good parenthood is the power of identifying oneself with a child, feeling his motives, realizing his limitations, but having no ulterior motive.

So far as I have observed the self-regulated child does not need any punishment. Punishment forms a vicious circle. A child is spanked; spanking is hatred and each spanking makes his hate more and more; so his behaviour gets worse and more spanking is applied. The result is a bad-mannered, sulky, destructive little hater, so innured to punishment that without it he would feel lonely, and thus he 'sins' in order to get some sort of emotion from his parents (a hate one will do when there is no love one); he is beaten, he repents . . . and begins again next morning. But the self-regulated child does not go through this hate cycle. He does not need to behave badly; he has no use for lying and breaking; his body has never been called filthy or wicked; he has not had occasion to rebel against authority or to fear his parents. Tantrums he will have but they will be short-lived and not tending to neurosis. My knowledge of anthropology is almost nil, but I am told that roughly there are two schools of thought about primitive man; one, that he was a savage, a killer, a wife-snatcher, a brute: the other, that he was peaceful, social, kindly. The adjectives used suggests the difference between the disciplined and the self-regulated child. Children when allowed to be themselves are peaceful and social and kindly. The view held by so many psychologists, especially the Freudians, that the inner man has to be restrained, disciplined, sublimated has no meaning to those who have seen free children. The fundamental difference between the Freudian school and Reich is simply the one I am examining now; Reich believes that life isn't evil, that the Unconscious isn't a devil, that all individual and social evils are man-made, made by interference with the life process; I do, however, know that, since some educators and parents do not interfere with the life process, adult interference is not a fixed and final attribute of human nature.

But punishment of children comes under the heading of adult interference with life itself. Facing the question frankly and openly we have to grant that most punishing stems from the irritation of adults simply because childhood is not young adulthood; children and grown-ups are in many ways antagonist in their interests. Our Summerhill dining-room is one big noise most of the time, so that the staff segregate themselves for their evening meal. Children have not got our adult values of material things, and much of parental anger is on account of tools and books and what not spoiled by neglect. Punishment, like jealousy, is very much the product of adult possessiveness.

ASN FC 63–4

The teacher, like the artist, the philosopher, and the man of letters, can only perform his work adequately if he feels himself to be an individual directed by an inner creative impulse, not dominated and fettered by an outside authority.

BR UE 159

Selective list of books written by the four educators dealt with here

NEILL, A. S.

1	*A Dominie in Doubt*	Herbert Jenkins, London	1920
2	*A Dominie Dismissed*	,,	
3	*The Problem Child*	,,	1926
4	*The Problem Parent*	,,	1932
5	*The Problem Teacher*	,,	1939
6	*That Dreadful School*	,,	1948
7	*The Free Child*	,,	1953
8	*Summerhill: A Radical Approach to Education*	Gollancz, London	1965
9	*Talking of Summerhill*	,,	1967

LANE, HOMER

NOTE: Lane wrote very little, and that little is inaccessible. This list includes the one book by Homer Lane, and other material by him appears in the two others cited.

1 *Talks to Parents and Teachers* Allen & Unwin, London 1928
2 Bazely, E. T. *Homer Lane and the Little Commonwealth,* Allen & Unwin, London 1948
3 Wills, W. David *Homer Lane, A Biography* Allen & Unwin, London 1964

KILPATRICK, W. H.

1	*The Project Method*	Teachers College, Columbia University, New York	1918, 1929
2	*Foundations of Method*	The Macmillan Company, New York	1925
3	*Education for a Changing Civilization*	The Macmillan Company, New York	1929
4	*The Educational Frontier*	The Century Co. New York	1933
5	*The Teacher & Society*	Appleton-Century, New York	1937
6	*Philosophy of Education*	The Macmillan Company, New York	1951, 1963

RUSSELL, B.

1 *Mysticism & Logic*	Allen & Unwin	1910, 1963
2 *Principles of Social Reconstruction*	,,	1916, 1960
3 *On Education*	Unwin Books	1926, 1964
4 *The Scientific Outlook*	Allen & Unwin	1931
5 *Education & the Social Order*	,,	1932, 1961
6 *Sceptical Essays*	,,	1935, 1948
7 *Unpopular Essays*	,,	1950
8 *Why I am not a Christian*	,,	1957

List of useful books

Archambault, R. D. (ed.) — *Philosophical Analysis & Education* Routledge & Kegan Paul, 1965

Boyd, W. & Rawson, W. — *The Story of the New Education*, Heinemann, 1965

Brauner, C. J. — *American Educational Theory*, Prentice-Hall, New Jersey, 1964

Brauner, C. J. & Burns, H. W. — *Problems in Education and Philosophy*, Prentice-Hall, New Jersey, 1965

Cremin, L. A. — *The Transformation of the School*, Vintage, New York, 1961

Hollins, T. H. B. (ed.) — *Aims in Education*, Manchester, 1966

Moore, E. C. — *American Pragmatism*, Columbia, New York, 1961

Oakeshott, M. J. — *Rationalism in Politics*, Methuen, 1962 (Essays entitled *The Voice of Poetry in the Conversation of Mankind*, and *The Study of Politics in a University*. c.f. the essay in *The Concept of Education* mentioned below.)

Park, J. — *Bertrand Russell on Education*, Allen & Unwin, 1964

Peters, R. S. — *Ethics & Education*, Allen & Unwin, 1966

Peters, R. S. (ed.) — *The Concept of Education*, Routledge & Kegan Paul, 1967

Reid, L. A. — *Philosophy & Education*, Heinemann, 1962

Richards, J. A. — *Philosophy of Rhetoric*, Oxford University Press, 1965

Tibble, J. W. (ed.) — *The Study of Education*, Routledge & Kegan Paul, 1966

Warnock, G. *English Philosophy since 1900*, Home University Library, Oxford University Press, 1963

White, M. (ed.) *The Age of Analysis*, Mentor, 1964

Wilson, J. *Language & the Pursuit of Truth*, Cambridge University Press, 1960

Wilson, J. *Thinking with Concepts*, Cambridge University Press 1960